Alberta Galla    Michele Buonsanti

# THE MOST BEAUTIFUL BEACHES IN CRETE

A Guide to hidden, picturesque locations
along the Cretan Coastline

D0067221

ISBN: 960-6655-11-3

**Published by:**

© MYSTIS

15, Kalisperidon str. – Heraklion – Crete
Tel. 2810 226518-346451 - Fax 2810 221908
e-mail: mystis@her.forthnet.gr

Graphic design: Giovanni Scattin

English translation by Stephen  Pastorello
Illustrations by Cristina Cazzanello
Photography by Michele Buonsanti

# INDEX

# THE MOST BEAUTIFUL BEACHES IN CRETE

A guide to hidden, picturesque locations
along the Cretan coastline

# INTRODUCTION

This guidebook, which has been compiled in the form of a travel diary, is the result of our explorations of the island of Crete in search of 'secret' beaches or, as indicated in the title, 'hidden', isolated beaches that can be considered as being definitely off the beaten track.

Crete has always been a favourite destination amongst travellers and tourists because of its mythological and historic charm and the fact that it is considered the cradle of Mediterranean civilisation. The island has of course also been explored and studied on account of its extremely beautiful landscape and natural characteristics. Along the northern side of the island, one will encounter alternating, mountainous, hilly and low coastal regions and long stretches of sandy coastline, while on the southern side, visitors will find high cliffs and dramatic scenery, indented coastlines with ravines and gorges and an endless number of small gulfs, inlets and coves at the edge of a natural and still intact, marine environment.

In recent years - and especially along the northern coast - with its countless hotel complexes and new residences, the ever-burgeoning tourist industry has been gradually occupying and devouring mile after mile of the coastline, which for centuries had been admired and described by European travellers charmed by such beautiful landscape.

Many of the 'hidden' beaches we describe on the following pages can be reached only on foot and are located at the end of deep gorges or secluded valleys. As many of them are totally isolated and provide no tourist amenities at all, we would advise visitors to procure a good map of the area they want to explore and some basic hiking kit and provisions. In many cases, along the impervious paths and at the sites we indicate you will find no snack bars: at these places you will feel you have become real explorers!

Many of the beaches listed are close to places of historic or religious interest and so we shall occasionally mention the presence of Minoan, Doric, Greek and Roman archaeological sites, and also churches dating back to the Byzantine period. We would draw the visitor's attention to the churches in particular as they bear witness to and help one comprehend more clearly the profound religious feelings that still permeate the entire island. Similarly, Venetian fortifications and castles are reminders of the long period during which Crete was a colony of the *Serenissima*.

Ideally, this is a guidebook for 'real travellers'; and by that we mean those visitors who will want to avoid the hordes of tourists and simply do their own thing. With such individuals in mind, we have prepared a selection of localities and attempt to provide the information they will need to get there. At the same time, our aim was to convey to the reader some of our own impressions on first discovering these fascinating places.

Only for the sake of completeness, our guidebook will also mention the 'famous' beaches - or, let's say, places that are not entirely 'hidden away' - in order to provide a thorough overview of the island's coastline.

In undertaking this work, we had no intention of trying to discover new seaside paradises and our sole aim was that of simply communicating our own experiences (as enthusiastic travellers) to people who still avoid 'doing it the easy way' and will never give in to the temptations of standard, 'all-in' package tours.

Dictynna

Gramvousa:
Balos beach

Ravdouchas

Phalassarna

Kastelli

Sfinari

Agios Mironas

Hrisoscalitissas

Amigdalokefali

Kandanos

Flafonissi

Gialos

Krios beach

Grammeno votsalo
beach

Paleohora

Gianiskari beach

Sougia

Lissos

# Western Crete

Stavros

Kalathas

Hania

Marathi

Koutallas

Kokkino Horió

Obrosgialos

Pajeloni

Vamos

Georgeoupoli

Lofka Ori

gia Roumeli

Agios Paulos

Marmara

Phinix

Gliká Nerá

Ilingas

Hora Sfakion

*Elafonissi*

# The beaches facing the Libyan Sea: from Hòra Sfakìon to Elafonìssi

We arrive at **Hòra Sfakìon** in the afternoon and the village is deserted. The morning excursionists have all taken the ferryboat over to Agia Rouméli, where, without making too much of an effort, they will want to spend time absorbing the beauty of the Samarià gorges. They will be back in the evening though, when they will start mingling with the real travellers, who can be easily identified by their knapsacks, hiking boots and their exhausted appearance after completing the seventeen-kilometre descent. We will find them all later on in the tavernas around the harbour in search of refreshment.

The village is spread out around a natural inlet below the surrounding mountainside. While the upper reaches of the village - a grey agglomeration of stone dwellings with a slightly abandoned appearance - form the oldest part, the most lively area is around the harbour, which is 'protected' by a hill covered in green cluster pines. At the top of the hillside we can make out the ruins of a castle dating back to the early years of the Venetian domination. Hòra Sfakìon is in any case not just a point of departure for trips into the mountain gorges: there are quite a few charming beaches very close at hand, and they can be reached either by boat or on foot.

We decide to ignore the pretty small beach tucked away just behind the harbour and travel on towards Anòpoli. After driving a few kilometres, we find a road sign that points in the direction of the beach at **Ilingas**. A brief descent along a rough road leads us to an open space in front of a taverna, where we decide to park. We continue on foot, walking down a flight of steps that lead to the sea. On this broad

*Glikà Nerà*

beach composed of sand, gravel and pebbles there are no leisure facilities. We notice a couple and their children, who are all wearing diving gear and seem to have just returned from an underwater expedition. Ilingas is located at the end of a small gorge and flanked by two high cliffs, in which we notice a few cavities and grottoes. The secluded coves nearby can be easily reached if you are in the mood for a short swim.

We make our way back to the main road and, after about one and half kilometres, as we are driving through an open bend, we notice the black and yellow, E4 Pan-European Footpath marker on a sign pointing in the direction of **Glikà Nerà.** The name of this locality means 'sweet waters' or 'fresh water', which is quite curious, and we are not sure what to expect. In any case, from this point we are able to see an inlet in the distance, which looks as if it will be an excellent place for an afternoon swim. Leaving our car, we walk down along a steep, uneven footpath that winds on between pinnacles of rock sheer above the sea and at a certain point, to our left, we are suddenly stunned by the panorama: standing above a broad, open slope, we stop to absorb the beauty of an incredible palette of colours created by the sea below us. The dark cobalt blue of the deeper water blends with patches of turquoise, at points where the sea is shallower, gradually fading into a lighter shade of emerald. It took us half an hour to get to the beach, and during that time we did experience a few moments of apprehension on account of the fact that at certain points the rough track seems to almost disappear above the precipice, leaving one entirely exposed above a frightening abyss. We would advise other travellers to proceed with great caution if they follow this route.

Although it is mid-October, we find quite a few people on the beach. It is not until quite some time later that we discover that Glikà Nerà can also be reached by a small boat that travels out from Hòra Sfakìon and that it is possible to hire deck chairs and umbrellas at a small snack bar that has been erected on the concrete blocks of the mooring jetty. Practically nothing detracts from the charm of this stretch of grey sand, where tamarisk trees offer adequate shelter from the heat of the sun. In the landward direction, the strand is surrounded by an enormous 'wall' of streaked, metamorphic rock and sharp pinnacles. The 'odd' attraction of Glikà Nerà however is the presence of a series of fresh-water pools marked by mounds of stones and protected by sheets of waxed tarpaulin. These water holes, which can be found practically all over the site, are obviously used by bathers when they want to cool off: in one of the largest some stone steps have been installed to help people enter the cool water. At the sandbar, the seabed slopes down steeply into deep water, which is very inviting and transparent on account of the pebble-strewn bottom. A short distance out to sea one will often notice passing canoes and dinghies, which are used by people to get to the many small deserted coves that can be found at the end of ravines along this part of the coast.

It is now a bit too late to walk any farther along the European footpath. After Glikà Nerà, its meandering course leads up to higher ground and then down again to Loutrò, and we know we would not have enough time to visit any of the other beaches nearby. After leaving Glikà Nerà, we drive past Anòpoli, a large village located on a fertile plain at an altitude of 600 m, and continue towards Aràdena. Just before an iron bridge that spans the Aràdena Gorge, a sign on the left-hand side of the road points in the direction of Livanianà and Phinix. Here, the mountain, which slopes down towards the sea, creates a desolate, almost 'lunar' landscape, and, after a kilometre of steep, sharp bends, we drive through Livanianà, a small, dilapidated ghost town which seems to cling as best it can to the sloping ground upon which it stands and is half-hidden amongst secular olive trees. It would appear the omnipresent black goats we notice are its only inhabitants. After another two and a half kilometres, we reach **Phinix,** a locality close to two delightful inlets. The village is separated from Loutrò by the Cape Kouros promontory. Looking seaward, the first bay, on the left, has a short, rocky strand, next to which we notice two small

*Phinix*

hotels on the sea front. It is possible to walk over to the bay on the right, which has a more solitary appearance and very clear water, in about ten minutes.

The next day, we leave Hòra Sfakìon in the late morning on a small ferryboat that takes us to Paleòchora. On this short trip, which we have always found enchanting, we pass by Loutrò, Agia Rouméli and Soùgia. It is a fascinating experience to slowly cruise along the coast so near to the impressive southern slopes of the Lefkà Ori, the White Mountains. We feel that we could almost reach out and touch them. Seen from the sea, the clearly visible course of the European Path follows the coastline, rising and descending on its way cross the mountain range. After about twenty minutes, the ferryboat stops at the small secluded harbour of Loutrò, with its one-storey buildings and dwellings and its quiet hotels, which create a harmonious, picturesque setting in which white, light blue and indigo are the predominant colours. We are sorely tempted to spend a few days in this peaceful haven. Nevertheless, we start off again after a short stop and once beyond the promontory, we sail past Phinix (which we have already mentioned) and the small inlet of **Marmara** at the end of the Aràdena Gorge. Marmara, characterised by the presence of smooth, white slabs of rock, is now hardly 'hidden' at all as it has become a favourite destination for day-trippers from Hòra Sfakìon. We now catch glimpses of other small, remote beaches before we begin to make out the church of Agios Paulos in the distance. The trip includes a rather long stop-off at **Agia Rouméli**, which is probably intended to allow the excursionists that have come down from the Samarià gorges to rest on the dark sand at the seafront before returning in the evening. It is curious to see the village strand disseminated with mountaineering gear, heavy boots, rucksacks and hiking sticks, while the owners of all this equipment lazily cool off in the water or stretch out on the sand to recover after so much physical exercise. This stop however finally gives us a chance to walk along a short stretch of the E4 footpath and visit **Agios Paulos,** one of the oldest churches on the island, which stands at the edge of a magnificent beach.

We leave the village and follow signs that point us in the direction of the European Footpath. We cross a riverbed, now waterlogged on account of the rain of the previous day, and, never losing sight of the sea, we continue for another six kilometres through small woods of cluster pine, along interminable stretches of land strewn with small rocks and boulders and small deserted bays. We occasionally come across some fairly impervious terrain, where it is difficult to walk, especially at points where the path crosses the sand dunes. After an hour and a half, we finally catch a glimpse of a building constructed

Agios Paulos

in the shape of a Byzantine cross: a very small structure of exquisite design with light marble facing and finished with red, grey and ochre-coloured stone elements. This tiny church dedicated to St. Paul is enchanting: also because - according to tradition - the Apostle Paul stayed here briefly before returning to Rome as a prisoner. We enter the church, which has been recently restored, only to find however that it contains very few fragments of frescoes on the vaults of the arches and in the cupola. We suddenly hear a stir outside and a voice asks us to leave the church: a large dinghy has suddenly landed on the beach and a false Saint Paul wearing a dark tunic and holding a curved stick comes ashore, followed by two cameramen! We walk away from the church to visit the adjacent beach covered in very fine, black pebbles and decide to go swimming in the deep water. It is so clear and transparent it seems we have fallen into the heart of a pure crystal. The magnificent scenery is marred only by the presence of a snack bar. Unfortunately, this is not just one of the usual one-storey buildings in concrete with a straw roof one often sees on the island: at the back of the structure we notice a very unsightly, abandoned prefabricated building.

After a few hours, we embark again at Agia Rouméli. The boat plies a constant course very near the coastline and we pass by rocky inlets, accessible only from the sea. We make an unforeseen landing at Tripitì, an almost impervious gorge, to discharge a pick-up truck laden down with small olive trees that belongs to a group of shepherds. Our map indicates an archaeological site close to this point, but the gorge is so narrow we wonder where it might be. After a short stop at the quay in **Soùgia**, a seaside resort spread out beside a long beach (with few leisure facilities), the next broad inlet – bordered by a shoreline of pebble-strewn sand surrounded by rocky peaks - is the one close to the archaeological site of **Lissòs**.

We pass Cape Flomes and the majestic gorges give way to the low, forest-covered mountains of the Selino region. In front of us, we now see the wide Selino Bay and its two beaches and can easily make out the harbour and the houses of **Paleòchora** bathed in the glowing colours of the sunset over on the far left-hand side. Despite the fact we are now well into Autumn, this graceful little town, once dominated by a Venetian hilltop fortress, is still very lively on account of the many tourists still milling through its streets. The beach at Paleòchora, which stretches on towards the western tip of the island, is a long strip of fine sand, upon which tourists will find various leisure facilities. We are more attracted however by the beaches within the Selino Bay proper. To reach these sites, the next day we travel along the

Sougia

recently-built coastal road, which, after the harbour, goes past the camping-site, and we follow the signs that indicate the beaches at **Gianiskàri** and **Anidri**. We are surrounded by low sandstone hills and thorny undergrowth as we travel four kilometres to two inlets that are separated by a row of small rocks which divide the long strand into two separate parts. Looking seawards, on the right-hand side there are umbrellas and deck chairs, all neatly arranged in rows on the sandy, pebble-strewn beach, while to the left, separated by a patch of Cretan rockrose, we find a long stretch of light-coloured, large-grain sand (mainly frequented by nudists) bordered by tamarisk trees. The whole area is well-kept and clean, and even the snack bars tend to go unnoticed. If one is looking for a very natural, seaside environment, this is it. The European Footpath is also very close and we would suggest you follow it as far as the western promontory (though not in the summertime!): the walk, which would take about an hour, is quite easy and the route well marked. At a few points this particular section of the footpath - very scenic and made more pleasant by the pervasive fragrance of Aleppo Pine - turns inland towards the mountain but it remains at a practically constant level. When we walked along it in December, the surrounding terrain was also coloured by the tiny pink flowers of plants that are similar to heather.

On the Koundoùra side, the beaches to the west of Paleòchora are all easily accessible. One after the other, we visited the beaches at **Psilos Vhrachos**, **Karavopetra** and **Kolpos Plakaki**: they are all located only a few yards below the coast road and are well marked. We thought the most attractive strand in this area however is the **Grammeno Votsalo** beach just before Gialos. At this beach of 'pebbles with patterns', a small headland, Cape Trachili, is surrounded by a magnificent cedar wood, which divides the strand into two parts, one of which is covered in sand and the other in pebbles. Visitors will find beach umbrellas on both sides and a number of sandy coves in the recesses of the promontory itself. The only unsightly element here is a long row of greenhouses located on the landward side of the beach, towards the Selino hills: their white plastic coverings definitely disturb the view. The principle economic activities in this area are tourism and agriculture, however both 'vocations' appear to culminate at **Cape Krios,** where the local crops grow in protected lots along the coast, close to a broad, tranquil strand.

From a road sign we learn that the Elafonìssi Beach is 14 kilometres from this point so we go back towards Gialos, driving along a road that winds across a series of gentle slopes covered by groups of freely-roaming sheep and goats. We gradually approach Sklavopoùla, a little village in the middle of nowhere, which is nevertheless certainly worth visiting. We discover there are three Byzantine churches here, one of which (Agios Georgeos) contains a series of precious frescoes produced by various painters from the year 1290 onwards. The asphalt road suddenly ends after Sklavopoùla and we find ourselves on a dirt road which suddenly winds over a dusty cross-weave of arid, undulating hills until we finally glimpse in the distance the white sandy coves of the Elafonìssi peninsula and the light blue sea. We gradually descend to a flat, lower level, where we are once again surrounded by greenhouses. Before visiting the famous Elafonìssi beach, we decide to explore the area and turn into a cart-road on our left, which leads towards the coast and the wide bay of Vroulias. As we drive into an open space, we notice a large quantity of burnt refuse in a wide circle of stones, which leaves us rather perplexed. Nevertheless, the panorama below us - a long green belt of coastline with small bays separated by rocks - is very inviting. At this point we are not quite sure whether or not we want to walk down to the sea along a nearby footpath as we are afraid we may come across more of these makeshift rubbish tips; but driven simply by curiosity, we stroll on and very soon we find we are back on the European Footpath. At regular intervals, we find special E4 signs, which invite hikers to always respect the natural environment and in particular to protect a wonderful cedar forest. A handwritten notice in Greek warns visitors that they should respect the ancient trees and that their branches should not be bent or dam-

*Elafonissi: the Cedar Beach*

aged in any way (it takes a whole year for them to grow just one centimetre, and the tree roots are very delicate). The anonymous author of these notices goes on to explain that, despite their appearance, the cedars have not dried up and they are still growing. Finally, he trusts that visitors will all spontaneously assume responsibility for their protection and informs us that it would only take a few years to destroy them and thousands of years to make them grow again.

Thus, we arrive at the sea and we decide to call this enchanting spot the **Cedar Beach**. We stop to rest a while. The scenery is splendid: the beach seems to be composed of a mixture of sand, fine shingle and minute fragments of shattered sea-shells, and the sea is transparent, also on account of the reflection of the sunlight on the flat,

*One of the many beaches on the Agia Roumeli-Sougia route*

*Gianiskàri sandy beach*

white, calcareous stone. Later on, we go swimming in the scintillating waters and are gently caressed by low waves and surrounded by thousands of tiny fish: the enchantment continues! We are surprised to notice that one of the submerged slabs of flat rock that we find on the gently-sloping seabed is almost perfectly square, and looks as if it were part of a submerged house (it even has a kind of seemingly man-made beading along the sides). It is now nearly one o'clock in the afternoon, and it's very hot; we are not exactly in a hurry to leave the water at this point. However, we look for a shady spot under the near-by cedar trees, the trunks of which - tormented by the sea wind and saline deposits - have become frayed and appear to be crumbling into fine, sharp 'blades'. The roots of these trees tend to curiously protrude above ground level. All around us there are silent signs of the silent presence of nature-lovers and solitary campers and the occasional excursionist who has decided to venture along this stretch of the European Footpath.

On returning to the point we started from, after a walk that takes about twenty minutes, we finally head off towards the **Elafonìssi Beach**. It is now late Autumn, however we get the impression we have suddenly inadvertently wandered into a funfair with all the 'fairground' noises. The beach is occupied by crowds of bathers, and every square centimetre of this beautiful strand seems to be covered with deck chairs, beach umbrellas and kiosks that distribute hamburgers and chips. Our sole advice to visitors would be that Elafonìssi should be visited in the off-season, when it is fairly certain there will not be many people around. However, at this locality - undoubtedly an attractive spot - you will find a splendid natural swimming pool of rare beauty and an authentic rainbow of colours, including the turquoise blue of the sea, white sand (on the island in front of the beach it is also tinged with the pink colouring of broken sea-shells), red rocks and the bright green colour of the cedars. Dare we suggest that this paradise has been unfortunately spoilt by mass tourism?

# The beaches in the far west: from Gramvousa to Chrisoskalìtissa

The Gramvousa promontory is the northern tip of the western part of the island. To reach the beach in the Gulf of Tigàni (commonly known as **Balos)**, you will have to drive through Kastelli Kìssamo, which has an attractive harbour, and five kilometres farther on, take a road on the right which passes through the village of Kalivianì and goes on to the Balos hotel. Until a few years ago, it would have been necessary to continue on foot from this point (a two and a half hour walk!), however the track has now been widened and transformed into a passable, dirt road. With an 'off-road' vehicle or a sturdy automobile, one can reach Balos (about 8 km) by travelling along this rough, uneven route that follows the crest of a long ridge, without losing sight of the verdant Rodopoù peninsula.

The slim and arid Gramvousa peninsula protrudes out into the Cretan Sea. After covering the first six kilometres, we stop to rest at the recently-built Agia Irini chapel. The presence of water here is a clue that leads us to discover in the midst of a thick oleander grove, an ancient, light-coloured, stone fountain now used only by herds of mountain goats that come here to quench their thirst and rest in the shade. At this point the vegetation is more luxuriant and forms a vast fuchsia-coloured blanket extending down to the sea. After another two kilometres, we reach a long, rocky plateau, where we are forced to abandon the car and continue on foot. At a tiny kiosk, where there is a superb view of the sea, we stock up with sandwiches and light drinks and start off on a footpath to our left. The track first winds up over the crest of Mount Geroskinos and then, after about 300 yards, reaches a point where the view is breathtaking. Around Tigàni Bay there is

Balos

a vast, irregular stretch of white sand, tinged here and there with a light reddish colour (perhaps created by traces of broken coral), at the end of which we notice a shallow lagoon coloured by undulating streaks of white and pink. After a fairly easy descent (20 minutes) along a flight of large stone steps, which leads us down to the white sand, we immediately go for a swim in this delightful 'tropical' sea. As the water gradually gets deeper, we notice how the light blue colour turns into a deep blue. At the centre of the bay and to the left (looking seawards) there are some large rocky islets that look as if some capricious deity once threw them there to make the landscape more sensational. On the left-hand side of the broad beach a small snack bar provides some shelter from the blinding sunlight, while over to the right we easily distinguish the shape of a fortress on the island of Gramvousa, which the Venetians called Grabuse.

Gramvousa was once an important outpost created to provide a form of defence against pirate raids. During the Venetian dominion, the castle, which was builty on the highest ground (137 m) contained the troops' living quarters and a church dedicated to The Annunciation. The island fortress can still be visited. The tiny island, which was self sufficient on account of its abundant water supply, was not ceded to the Turks until 1715 (more than forty years after the fall of Crete). Gramvousa is now visited by tourists, who reach the island by boat from Kastelli Kίssamo. As we observe the island, we actually see one of the small ferries turning back into the bay, where it will stop for a while to let the more agile day-trippers dive off into the water for a quick swim.

It is early May. The beach is half deserted and our visit to Balos has been a very pleasant experience. We realise however that on a midsummer's day these beaches may not be quite so charming!

**Phalàssarna** is on the western side of Gramvousa. Here, you will find a beach with splendid white sand and an important archaeological site that extends as far as the shore. Over the years, Phalàssarna has undergone considerable change: now a popular destination for tourists, it has become a lively centre with many bars, tavernas, holiday homes and hotels. Its various agricultural activities have also been developed and the splendid adjacent terrain is now covered with olive plantations and greenhouses (which seem a little incongruous in such beautiful surroundings). Located below the western slopes of the Gramvousa peninsula and Mount Geroskinos, Phalàssarna offers a succession of tiny embayments. Those of interest are the so-called 'large inlet', a smaller, secluded inlet below the *Galazià Thea* taverna (the name of the restaurant means 'celestial panorama'), and, farther north, a cove in a vast area close to the site of a city-state of the Hellenistic period.

We now drive on back towards the south, in the direction of the village of Sfinàri, looking for other secluded spots. We decide to leave the main road at a point about 4 km after the village of Plàtanos and find one just by chance at the end of a dirt track (1.5 km from the main road). After arriving in a clearing where there is a small church, we follow the dried-up bed of a small stream through a gorge full of ferns, wild shrubs and oleander and find a beach of dark sand. This unmarked spot can be reached in about fifteen minutes.

**Sfinàri** is a quiet spot located by an inlet protected by the luxuriant slopes of the Korakas promontory. The sand and gravel beach can be reached by following the signs that lead down to a few tavernas (which prepare meals with very fresh fish) and a free-camping area. The strand is bordered by enormous, shady tamarisk trees, and, also on account of its position, we felt it was an ideal spot for a swim just before sunset. At this time of day, the sea is ablaze with the golden reflections of the setting sun and one can hear the pleasant sound of a brook flowing close to the beach.

The coast road leads on in the direction of Elafonìssi, but we decide to stay focused on the beaches around **Amigdalokefàli**. Just outside the village, on the right, a fine road winds on for about eight kilometres towards **Livadìa**, a hamlet close to a series of rocky inlets bordered by black sand, where we understand it would be rather difficult to swim. Definitely more attractive is the tiny beach at **Agios Mìronas**, a little farther on to the south: this spot can be reached by turning left at a point about 1 km along the same track. We find that the pebble-strewn beach is surrounded by rocks and very secluded, even though a couple of recently-built tavernas high up on the right-hand side would suggest that this will not be such a peaceful environment for much longer.

Continuing in the same direction, we pass by Stòmio and, after a few more kilometres, reach the Chrisoskalìtissa Convent, which stands directly above the sea on a high rocky spur, its candid structure resembling a mysterious fortress. A curious local legend reports that one of the steps leading to the entrance of the convent is made of pure gold but is visible only to those whose souls are untainted by sin. We decide to climb up the steep stairway, however noticing not even the dimmest trace of gold but only the blinding whiteness of the stone from which the steps were hewn. It gradually dawns upon us that we are a pair of incorrigible sinners!

# The beaches at Kìssamo and Hanià: from the Rodopoù peninsula to the Bay of Kalìves

The enormous mass of the Rodopoù peninsula stretches out between the Gulfs of Kìssamo and Hanià and is practically uninhabited in the northernmost part. As we see on our map, only one road, with a narrow, white carriageway, leads out to Cape Skala.

We have made the journey out to this farthest western tip of the island at the end of October, with the sun only faintly dimmed by haze and in the soft light that only Autumn days can offer. We intend to visit at Cape Skala, a magnificent bay which local people call **Dìctynna**. The name of this place, which is dotted with the ruins of a Greek-Roman temple (the Dictynnaion), is reminiscent of a Cretan goddess: according to legend, after king Minos had threatened to seduce her, the huntress-nymph Dìctynna threw herself into the sea to escape her impulsive suitor but was promptly saved by nets cast by some fishermen. The Greek word for 'net' is *dikti* (diktu).

In the past, one would have had to walk an entire day to reach Dìctynna; nowadays, this barren and yet beautiful and uncontaminated promontory can be reached by driving along a fairly uneven dirt road, which starts at the village of Rodopoù. Note that for such trips it is advisable to procure a reasonably solid vehicle, preferably of the 4-wheel drive type. Before starting off on this route, we stop for a moment at Rodopoù, where there is a Venetian villa that dates back to the 14th century. We discover that its recent restoration was limited to the main load-bearing elements and structure of the building. The villa, which stands in the upper part of the main square, on the right-hand side, has an attractive *piano nobile*, decorated with a beautiful window and pediment, however it is not yet possible to visit the inside. We stop at the *kafeneion* close by to see if we can gather more

*Gramvousa*

information about this old building but none of the elderly gentlemen sitting at the tables drinking their first morning coffee can tell us the name of the Venetian family to whom the fertile surrounding land had been assigned.

We drive on and, starting just outside the village, for about a kilometre, we see an expanse of low vineyards and vegetable plots extending back from the dirt road. The road traverses the upper ridge of the peninsula, where we find alternating sequences of large sheep pens and flat, green areas where other neat rows of grape vines are cordoned off by fences. As we reach higher ground, the Mediterranean *maquis* begins to take over, and the landscape is now characterised by the presence of thorny oaks, carob trees, Phoenician juniper and Cretan rockrose shaped by the wind. Suddenly, we also find a series of curious, pinnacle-shaped concretions. After travelling on a further 6 km, we reach an altitude of 600 m above sea-level. At the highest point, a turning to the left indicates the church of Agios Ioannis (St. John's church), in which, on the 29th August, the inhabitants of nearby towns and villages gather to celebrate the baptism of all newborn children of the same name. We continue, following a sign pointing towards the Dìctynna Sanctuary, and passing extensive grassy patches partially flooded by recent rainfall and now full of large pools of water, while curious goats begin to come close to our car as we drive along. Along the entire route, the only other vehicles we come across are a few pickup trucks driven by shepherds, and we see no other tourists at all. Eleven kilometres farther on, a road sign to the right points towards Meniès and the church of Agios Georgeos, which are part of an ancient monastery, the mediaeval tower of which is now visible in the distance. We now also catch a glimpse of the sea, as the downward stretch of road becomes steep and uneven. To be on the safe side, we leave our vehicle safely parked under a low hill. At this altitude of just 200 m above sea level, we are surprised to notice amongst thorny euphorbia shrubs a few pink cyclamen (a Cretan species that blossoms at the end of September), which the bramble-bushes have miraculously saved from the voracious herds. From this high point, we also begin to see the Dìctynna anchorage. Between two high walls of rock, it seems to have emerged from a deep cleft in the coastline. Having now descended closer to the beach, we come across more sheep folds at the edge of a vast archaeological area that surrounds the bay, which on the right-hand side terminates at a crop of high ground where the Dictynnaion once stood. The historian Strabone tells us that this building, which was built on the ruins of a temple dating back to the 7th century BC, was so large that it could be seen all across the western part of the island! The only remaining visible traces of the sanctuary are sections of grey marble, Ionic and Corinthian columns left lying in disarray on the ground. The enormous marble ruins are left abandoned, but fortunately a headless statue of Dìctynna the Huntress with her bloodhound was recovered and removed to the Archaeological Museum of Hanià.

The beach, surrounded by a wide, high crown of rocks, seems to have been created inside a natural amphitheatre. Formed by gravel and tiny pebbles, it is not very clean - perhaps on account of the fact it is not only frequented by fishermen but (during the high season) also by tourists, who come here from Kolimbàri by boat. Just beyond the sand-bar, the sea is filled with large, smooth, light-coloured rocks and the seabed falls away steeply into deep, transparent water filled with rich marine flora and sea creatures. At Dìctynna, the archaeological site creates an unforgettable suggestive appeal. On leaving this site, one final vision remains in our memory: that of a skinny, black, solitary goat moving silently along the seashore. He immediately took possession again of this corner of his habitat as soon as we moved away from the beach.

We took about an hour to get to Dìctynna (a distance of 18 km). If you decide to spend the day there, we would advise you to take supplies of food and water. It is possible in any case to find some shade under the tamarisk trees and sit on make-shift, very ancient-looking stone seats.

In the rocky, western part of the Rodopoù promontory there is only a strand called **Ravdoùchas Beach**, which is clearly sign-posted at the junction with the road that leads to Aspra Nerà on the Kastelli-Hanià national highway. After passing through Ravdoùchas, which is located in a beautiful position overlooking the sea, we turn off onto the wind-

*Diktynna*

ing, country road that leads down to the coast (2 km). At the side of a small harbour we find a fairly short stretch of sand and pebbles, protected on the landward side by a thicket of tall canes. The place has an unfortunately desolate appearance and is spoilt by the presence of rubbish of every imaginable kind scattered everywhere. We try to think of possible reasons for such neglect, which is contradicted by the presence of a few holiday homes, and we cannot imagine anyone might want to make use of this unkempt stretch of shore unless they choose it as a base for fishing expeditions.

We stop at Kolimbàri, a seaside resort with a recently constructed harbour, an interesting Sea Museum and the Gonià Monastery, which dates back to the 16$^{th}$ century and stands on the peninsula like a solitary fortress. From Kolimbàri, one will find along the entire coastline leading to Hanià various sandy beaches, which attract large numbers of bathers and visitors. From the beautiful city of Hanià, which still clearly bears witness to its Venetian past and where, on the western side of the Venetian port there is the long beach of Néa Chòra (well-equipped for tourists), we drive on to the Akrotiri promontory. Here, the small bays of **Stavròs**, **Kalathàs** and **Maràthi** are frequented by Hanià residents in the summer months and are thus also well-equipped with leisure facilities. They are also very crowded however. We go on looking for our 'hidden' beaches and, after leaving the city, we believe we have identified one in the bay of Kalìves, after Almirìda, in a small inlet called **Koutallas** (in the direction of Cape Drapanon). The presence of new holiday homes, which are currently in the process of being built or completed and are obsessively advertised on local advertising

*Koutallas*

placards, makes us think again: the Gulf of Kalìves, which is very pleasant and offers two very interesting beaches at Kalìves and Almirìda, will soon be utterly transformed by the massive development projects in progress. Nor will the building industry and developers fail to notice the green hilly area that leads out to the promontory. In the very near future the villages of Plaka and Kokkino Horiò will be crowded and we wonder whether the small pebble-covered inlet of Koutallas, locked in between two high flat rocks will actually offer enough space for the masses that will want to go there to swim.

We now climb up towards Cape Drapanon to explore another beach indicated on our map: **Obròsgialos**. Immersed in luxuriant countryside, the road rises as it passes through various localities and leads on to Palelòni, a hillside hamlet with pretty, restored stone houses surrounded by chestnut trees. After this little village, a road sign points towards Obròsgialos, which, after four kilometres of descending bends that take us through an area of open *maquis*, turns out to be just a mooring spot. However, the site is definitely rendered quite spectacular by the indigo-coloured water that gets very deep immediately beyond the shoreline. The place would be of little interest to landlubbers.

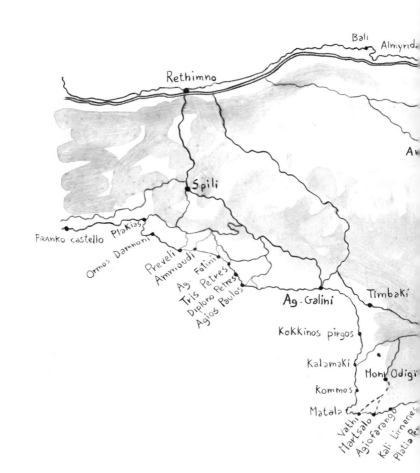

# Central Crete

Agia Pelagia
Lygaria

Heraklion Amnisos

Agii Deka

Ano Viannos

Pirgos

Lendos
Trypiti
Ag. Ioannis
Tris ekklisies
Ag. Nikitas
Maridaki
Tsoutsouros
Keratokampos
Arvi
Tertsa
Mirtos

Agios Nikitas

# The beaches to the west of Ieràpetra: from Mìrtos to Agios Nikìta

Fourteen kilometres beyond Ieràpetra, the coastal highway comes to an end at **Mìrtos**, a tranquil seaside resort frequented by local tourists and travellers. In the village, there are a few tavernas on the seafront, and we imagine they would probably offer very good fish dishes; we discover however the local preference is lamb roasted on the spit and typical Cretan food. In this little town, the beach, which faces the Libyan Sea is a long strand composed of dark sand and small pebbles. It resembles the stretches of coastline we will soon find two and a half kilometres farther on, at **Vathos** and **Kallikovrahtis.**

At **Tertsa**, in a small bay, there are some very tall tamerisk trees and a tiny restaurant beside a beach divided up by monolithic rocks that create small inlets. One hundred yards farther west, we stop at one of these well-kept coves, where we find a pleasant wooden structure around which we see a large bustling group of young people. We are told that this stretch of coastline is reserved (we fail to understand whether permanently or temporarily) for a group of journalists who are guests of a Japanese car manufacturer! The reporters, who have been commissioned to comment on a sort of promotional tour, definitely have at their disposal a fine beach where they can rest and swim in a wonderful setting.

From Tertsa, we drive along a dirt road that follows the uneven coastline, in an area characterised by its many greenhouses that are used to grow various types of vegetables. We pass through Psariforada and Sidonia, two villages which offer the usual temptations, tavernas and rooms to let, and through **Arvì**, another small rural centre with a recently-constructed harbour and beaches of no great beauty. Finally, we visit **Keratòcampos,** which has a small quay for fishing boats.

*Tertsa*

*Near Tsoùtsouros*

We are a little disappointed by the rather neglected state of the nearby beaches and by the fact the sea cannot be easily reached (on account of large boulders and rocks that emerge from the sea all along the shore), so we travel on to **Tsoùtsouros**, a pleasant little village, which lies beneath an imposing mountain rich in vegetation. The village is beside a sand and pebble beach, beyond which we notice very transparent water. Here too, the tourist trade seems to cater mainly for local clients, as is confirmed by the amiable young owner of a café where we stop to have a rest. Aris tells us that the recently-completed landing jetty is only equipped to accommodate small fishing vessels. We also learn that from out at sea, when the weather is fine, it is possible to see the columns and the perimeter of the ancient city of Inatos (one of the hundred cities described by Homer), renowned in antiquity for its hospitality. Our friend tells us that after Tsoùtsouros, if we walk along a footpath just above the beach, we can get to Maridaki and then the Monastery of Agios Nikìta in about ten minutes: sites that in his opinion are quite enchanting. Attracted by the prospect of discovering little-known locations along the coast, we decide to drive there, going up through the Kofinas mountain chain along a road that is very rough but offers beautiful panoramic views of the lower land. At an altitude of almost 1000 m, there is a 360° view across the surrounding area. At over 500 m above sea level, the landscape becomes a solitary 'moonscape', and the low rocky crags are surrounded by a myriad of colours: the vivid yellow of thorny euphorbia, the tiny purple and white flowers of the Greek horehound plant (*ballota acetabulosa*), and the violet, spherical blossom produced by thistles. Far below us, groups of oleander trees, which grow freely in well-

*Near Tsoùtsouros*

irrigated narrow valleys can be clearly seen, creating very visible streaks of green and intense pink. We encounter no-one along this road and our only company are the small flocks of sheep and agile goats. They wander around seeking shelter from the sun and group together in rock clefts, where the stone is curiously streaked with fine, black and white lines. Very soon, the ever-winding road begins to descend towards the sea and, although we have only travelled six kilometres, the countless bends make it seem we have been travelling for ages. On reaching a junction, we follow the road that leads to Agios Nikìta and Maridaki (6 km and 5 km, respectively). We are now quite close to the sea and in the ravines of Mount Kremastì the oleander has suddenly been replaced by tall palm trees that are bunched together and seem to tell us we are close to some exotic oasis. The typical Cretan palm trees (*phoenix Theophrastii*), now protected by European laws, grow in sandy soil in gorges very close to the sea. There are many exemplars at Vài in the eastern half of the island.

We reach the small monastery of Agios Nikìta, which stands sheer above the sea and which, for the last twenty-five years, has been in the sole custody and care of a little *kalogero* (monk). Enchanted by the number of flowers, fruit groves and olive trees, and also by the care and skill with which the surrounding slopes have been transformed into terraces to facilitate cultivation, we loudly exclaim that we have arrived in paradise. As we do so, a young monk with a hieratic look contradicts our belief with a sibylline comment of his own proffered in perfect English, suggesting that we are rather in hell (we fear he might be referring to the nudism practised just a short distance away!), and he points towards the beach, which is just beyond a gate outside the convent. It is quite likely that the monks, in ages past, entered and moored their boats in the bay and reached the monastery by walking up the high steps carved out of the rock and other smaller steps created in this vast area. The **Agios Nikìta** inlet, protected on the left by a high wall of lava rock, is bordered with gravel and tiny pebbles and surrounded by rocky crags that provide ample shade on very hot days. We shall always remember our experience here on a warm afternoon at the beginning of June on account of the incredible beauty of the sea, where we went for a swim in emerald-coloured water that turns a deep blue as the depth of the water increases. On our return, we stop again to chat with the young monk. He has a kind of 'foreign' look about him, but he certainly seems elegant in his dark costume and cylindrical hat, in stark contrast with the typical shabby attire that most monks would appear in. After asking us whether we like the beach, he tells he has come to Crete from Mount Athos in the Chalcidice Peninsula for a short holiday. We exchange addresses and invite him to come to visit us at our home in Elounda, however informing him also that he will not find the same peace and quiet there as in Agios Nikìta. We visit the rupestrian church, which is very interesting and filled with icons, expressing to our little *kalogero* our marvel at his considerable tolerance in allowing tourists to pass through a sacred place to get to the beach below. The gentle creature ensures us however that he is not disturbed at all by the visitors, who somehow alleviate his solitude.

After leaving Agios Nikìta, our next destination is another delightful site only a short distance away. **Maridaki** is a small group of houses tucked away in a mountain hollow, through which a stream flows under the shade of numerous oak trees. At this pretty site, we also find oleander trees and can smell the unmistakeable, bitter fragrance of fig trees. Located in an isolated bay, Maridaki is a charming location (like those often found in old post-cards) with its panorama and appealing shoreline, a couple of boats anchored in the inlet and no trace of tourist operators or their clients.

*Tris Ekklisies*

# The beaches below the southern slopes of the Asteroussia mountains

To the south of Heràklion, a fast, easy road leads down towards the southern part of the island (passing through towns and villages, the occupants of which are very evidently dedicated to winegrowing) and the green heart of the fertile Messarà plane, which extends as far as Pìrgos. Here, the imposing Asteroussia mountain chain forms a rocky barrier that protects beaches along the southern coastline which are certainly not 'famous', are difficult to reach without a good four-wheel-drive vehicle and have to be visited one by one as there are no direct links between them.

From Pìrgos we travel on to Hàrakas, a hamlet with an interesting fortress, and we follow the asphalt road as far as Parànifi. At the end of this village, a road sign on the left points towards Tris Ekklisìes. We drive on for 8 km along a road that is all ups and downs as it passes through the barren Asteroussia mountains, where, despite the arid environment, vast plots of land have been cultivated with vineyards and olive trees. Travelling along a fairly broad dirt road with a panoramic view of the sea, we drive towards **Tris Ekklisìes**, which once upon a time could only be reached on foot. A frantic desire to modernise everything has brought about many changes and the original character of this fishing village with its one-storey houses has been spoilt. It seems to have been transformed into a wild, and incomprehensible agglomerate of houses, where new buildings are constructed over older ones. Many of these edifices are often only slightly older then the new structures but are already in an advanced state of decay or have been abandoned. We also see a daring construction in metal, which is perhaps the shell of a new hotel.

We are disconcerted by this architectural anarchy and the 'wounds' we see inflicted on the otherwise enchanting, coastal landscape. It's a sad sight. Nevertheless - and never discouraged - we leave the village, taking a road that rises up to the left, and there in front of us we find a really beautiful beach composed of dark sand, stretching out for about 300 yards and protected on the eastern side by a high cliff. It looks like a natural amphitheatre with sharp crags looming above it and bordered on the western side by an enormous mass of rock. The surrounding terrain is coloured by the tiny pinkish flowers of aromatic thyme and covered by olive and carob trees. When we visit this site in mid-June, the beach is deserted and swept by strong northerly winds, which almost seem capable of forcing back the sea. The water here is clean and transparent and beyond the shoreline the seabed falls away immediately into deep water, in which the underwater crevices and caverns are inhabited by sea creatures of every kind.

We drive back down to Hàrakas, quickly passing by the other localities we find strung out beneath the mountain. From Vagionià we quickly reach Vassilikì and from there follow the signs to Lendas. After another 1.5 km, we turn left at a junction and go towards Krotos and the beach at **Trìpti**. Gradually rising, the territory we pass through presents a terrain with soft, gentle contours but it also becomes barren and rocky. We drive on past the little church dedicated to Agia Paraskevì and then an immense olive plantation and a series of low farm sheds constructed in sheet metal and concrete. Judging by the foul smell they emanate, they are probably used for chicken breeding. From this point on, the journey is a constant zigzag and definitely more difficult. For about six kilometres we drive along the side of a canyon formed by orange-colour rock faces until we finally enter the gorge proper. The landscape in the last part of the trip is so impressive that it reminds us of sensations we felt when we passed through the *sideròportes* ('iron doors') of the Samarià gorges to the south of Hanià. Two almost vertical cliffs loom above the very narrow trail, which, beyond a small oleander wood, leads down to the sea. Before arriving at the shore we find indicated on our left the small, now abandoned, Minoan archaeological site of Trìpti. A few one-storey buildings, a taverna (called 'Mathì') and the presence of boats and caravans suggest the place is frequented by local, weekend excursionists (it should be noted that Tripti can be reached in a much less adventurous manner from the nearby village of Lendas). The inlet is formed by a spacious semi-circular strand composed of sand and pebbles, with broad, barren, open hillside slopes and the sharp crags of the ravine in the background. In a very steep precipice to the right of the beach, there are two caverns, the shapes of which are reflected in the clear, light-green sea water beneath them, and some quite singular, metamorphic rock formations which look as if they might have been drawn with a pantograph.

# The beaches from Màtala to Lendas

At the end of the 1960s, European hippies who longed to find a totally 'free' environment found what they were looking for in Crete, in the three 'magical' villages of Màtala, Préveli and Vài.

Of these three localities, only **Màtala** seems to have preserved certain former ideal conditions as the village appears to have withstood the inexorable impact of the tourist boom, which occurred on account of its growing international fame. Nowadays, its suggestive grottoes overlooking the sea (actually inhabited by the 'flower children' at one stage), are protected and may be accessed only if one pays a small entry fee. Nevertheless, going for a swim on the beautiful beach nearby (a broad strand shaded by enormous eucalyptus trees) is still a unique experience. The charm of Màtala can be felt especially in the early evening, when the day-trippers have left and one can stroll in peace along the streets of the village; and even nowadays, it is not hard to find a few eccentric characters (perhaps now in their sixties and sporting long, grey hair) that run little art shops or small restaurants and seem to be quite content to have never left this place.

The village itself has ancient origins. In a report to the Venetian Senate in 1630, Francesco Basilicata, a high-ranking administrator of the *Serenissima*, described the church dedicated to the Holy Virgin in Màtala and its mosaic paving and a Greek inscription which reminded visitors to the church that they were entering sacred precincts: "*Lavate il capo et mondate li piedi, intrate poi in questa casa divina*" ["Wash your head and clean your feet before entering this sacred place."]. The building Basilicata referred to is probably the Panagia church, which is located beneath the grottoes and can still be visited.

If travellers feel like stopping over for a few days (perhaps not during the high season), they will definitely be captivated by the charm of this little place, which has no large hotels but only well-kept board-

Kokkini Ammos

ing houses run by sensible owners. The colourful balconies of these modest establishments, where clients always get a very friendly service, are often embellished by the intense shade of bougainvillea.

Naturally, the Màtala beach is always very crowded (especially in summer); so, if you like free, open, uncontaminated spots, it will only take you half an hour on foot to reach the charming 'red beach'.

This spot can be reached very easily. Just go in the direction indicated by the sign in the village itself ('**kòkkini ammos'** in Greek). Once outside the village, follow the lane bordered by tall, purple thistles and walk past an archaeological site overgrown with wild sage on the right-hand side. Then, a large fig tree with twisted branches indicates where you have to clamber up a short, steeper part of the track. Visitors will have to be cautious when they follow this footpath (use footwear a little more robust than simple sandals), which winds up to the top of a steep, rocky hill and then descends towards the sea. Before you get to the beach, which at first sight may seem entirely deserted, you will notice two low, rather dilapidated buildings decorated with some colourful mural artwork (the enormous, mysterious eye is rather curious). At this magnificent site, you will find a long, wide strand composed of soft, ochre-coloured sand. In the early morning, you may also discover that the beach is covered with tiny holes and marks that indicate the presence of loggerhead (caretta caretta) turtles that arrive during the night to lay their eggs.

Around midday, other excursionists come down from the hill, while at about just the same time, a lifeguard/beach-attendant arrives on a small boat to hire out beach umbrellas and deck chairs. It looks as if the so-called 'red beach' will never be crowded however: it is large enough to provide a secluded spot for everyone, and the nudists would certainly not complain. As we swam in the clear water, the current carried us beneath the high cliff at the western end of the inlet. Here, we found many craggy formations above water level, which seem to have been 'sculpted' by an artist: in these curious forms we seem to be able to identify the shapes of fantastic beasts, semi-human creatures such as the sphinx and a variety of esoteric symbols. We feel slightly envious of people who have had the opportunity to spend so much time in this idyllic environment and have fun creating these bizarre sculptures.

From Màtala, after driving through the village of Pitsìdia and continuing for another two kilometres, we take the turning on the right which leads to Siva and the Odigitria monastery. Siva is a small hillside village with a sort of 'cosy' atmosphere. The houses here are all made of stone and, around the large central square (the hub of social life for the villagers), hospitable tavernas offer such specialities as roast pigeon or goat's head. From here, the road leads up to Lìstaros, a village with a rather desolate appearance, perhaps due to the fact it reveals evident signs of a fire that recently raged wildly all around its perimeter and across the nearby countryside, consuming acres and acres of olive trees. The landscape has a sort of eerie appearance: we could see that entire olive plantations had been destroyed, but a few trees were spared or only half-burnt, which meant the fire had obviously capriciously followed an irregular course. It also seems that the fire miraculously stopped at the doors of the convent of Odigitria (literally, 'the Madonna who indicates the way'). This building, dating back to the 14$^{th}$ century, has the form of a fortress with a square outer rampart. An inner tower is very conspicuous in the courtyard dominated by the church dedicated to the Virgin Mary. The guardian of the monastery accompanies us inside the building, which is covered with ancient frescoes and icons, and swears that the Madonna worked a miracle. Not a single tree or flower had been touched by the flames, which, facilitated by a westerly wind, devastated the surrounding land for two whole days.

From Odigitria we follow the road signs to **Agiofàrango**, the 'gorge of the saints'. After driving along a fairly easy dirt road for about four kilometres, we come across a sign with a detailed 'historic' and geographical map of the area that informs us we must now continue on foot. Wearing hiking boots and with a provision of water and food, we walk on along a gradually descending riverbed: a track made slippery in parts by numerous slimy patches. We are accompanied along the way by the tinkling bells of a small herd of goats some way above, all lined up above the cavities in the ochre-coloured walls of the gorge, seeking shelter from the still very warm October sun. We walk on for a

*Agiofàrango*

good half hour between these suggestive rock walls of the gorge, surrounded by vegetation in which we recognise large quantities of thyme, the chaste tree plant (*agnus castus*), and here and there, the tall, undulating, solitary sheaves of squill (*urginea maritima*), a flower that traditionally heralds in the Autumn. Very gradually, the imposing landscape of the ravine acquires a less dramatic appearance, and the high rocky walls become less impervious. After making our way through a wood of pink oleander, we enter an open space with wooden benches close to an old church. This is not just another simple votive chapel, but a church in the true sense, which dates back to the 14th century and is dedicated to Saint Anthony. The building presents the cruciform layout typical of Byzantine churches and has red cupolas and a beautiful facade with an ogival-shaped, Gothic portal and a rose window. The building is also decorated with a large cross formed by the insertion of semi-circular majolica tiles. A well just beside the church offers us an occasion to fill our canteens with drinking water. In low, surrounding concretions there are numerous caves, where the hermits of this area once lived, while high above, to the left of the church, there is the *Igoumenospilio*, an enormous grotto with an opening in the ceiling, where the hermits gathered once a year. It is curious to think that the only way of knowing whether any of their brethren had died was by waiting to see whether all the stone seats inside the cavern would be occupied: if one of them was left empty, then the holy man who had the right to occupy it had most likely passed away. We walk on for a few hundred yards and finally the deep blue line of the sea comes into view and we notice a group of goats walking through the water along the shore.

It is a rather long strand, composed of sand and pebbles, and practically deserted if it were not for a naked gentleman with a long, grey beard, who emerges from the sea and quickly runs across to a primitive beach hut made of branches and leaves. At the far western end of the beach there is a cliff which joins the walls of the gorge to form a natural arch. We go swimming in the warm water, which is oddly cloudy, perhaps on account of the rain that fell the previous day. After a few hours other tourists arrive. In some crevices we notice a few beach umbrellas perhaps left by people who come here frequently. The presence of numerous large caverns stimulates our imagination, and we begin to wonder whether Agiofàrango is still inhabited by anchorites: this location has always been considered a very spiritual place and the mildness of the climate would allow anyone to live here all year round. It is even said that birds never migrate from this spot and remain here even during the winter.

We continue our exploration of the surrounding area and later, as we return to Odigitria, we find another side road that takes us towards Martsàlo and Vathì, two localities which really do have 'hidden' beaches that are well worth visiting. **Martsàlo** can be reached by driving five kilometres along a rough but passable road that winds through the hills and valleys. When we reach a small, recently-built, whitewashed church with fine bright yellow bordering, we are forced to leave our car and start walking. We follow the signs for the Martsàlo monastery. The footpath rises up over the rock, and then descends steeply towards the rupestrian church. We walk down some large irregular steps and are protected from falling off the precipice by a simple iron guard-rail. The church, dedicated to the Dormition of the Virgin, was dug out of the rock face and inside, in front of the icon of the Madonna, there are many *ex voto* offerings. Outside, lined up one beside the other, we find a few uninhabited cells. Passing through a gate that opens onto the abandoned kitchen garden of the convent, we look for a pathway that might lead to the lower ground below, but fail to find one. In the end, we give up and decide to follow a faintly-marked track that has been created by a large roving flock of sheep now resting lower down in the shade of a small but very tall group of palm trees towering above some olive trees and oleander. We reach the sea after a rather difficult, forty-five minute walk through dense, intricate patches of bright pink rockrose, in a silence broken only by the sound of the watchful goats stealthily moving through the green undergrowth. Martsàlo is a long, narrow stretch of sand and boulders: again, unfortunately ruined by the presence of rubbish tips. The presence of a makeshift quay created by a long sturdy tree trunk anchored to a large, semi-submerged boulder suggests that

*Martsàlo*

the place is periodically frequented by fishermen, who reach this spot from the sea. The deep, transparent water is very inviting.

Evening is now drawing on: we walk back up the valley, go past the convent and then drive on towards **Vathì**. To reach the place, after four kilometres we pass through two gates (probably used to keep sheep from wandering too far off) and follow a small, very steep, poorly-maintained road flanked on the right-hand side by a high wall of sandstone. We catch glimpses of the sea and, after another kilometre, notice a small, mustard-colour villa and then a small complex of holiday homes. At this point, we have arrived. It is a good idea to leave your vehicle here as the dirt road comes to an end. From here on, there is just a simple track that leads through the canebrakes and over the scattered rocks of a dried-up riverbed. A short distance before the Vathì inlet, on the left, there is a small snack bar. From here, we walk out onto a delightful beach of fine, light sand, where two wooden boats have been drawn up in front of a thicket of canes. The little bay has a rather particular conformation as there are various rocky recesses, low grottoes and a promontory which impedes a direct view of the open sea and generates the impression that one is standing on the shore of a mountain lake. We are about eight kilometres away from the junction at the Odigitria monastery; although the sun is now already setting, we go for a swim while the last rays of sunlight intensify the colour of the burnt hills, bathing them in a deep red light.

Leaving the Odigitria convent, we drive on to **Kalì Limenes**. The rough dirt road winds on for about fourteen kilometres across barren terrain inhabited only by dispersed flocks of sheep and takes us back to the southern slopes of the Asteroussia mountains. We had already

*Vathi*

seen an attractive print of Kalì Limenes produced in 1618 by the Venetian cartographer Francesco Basilicata, who, in a quaint, simple style, drew with vivid colours a broad inlet protected on the right-hand side by a headland (in light-blue), which he called the *Punta San Nicolò*. The print also shows a quite spacious strand with anchored galleons in front of it (painted in orange) and a series of tiny, dark-grey rocks, jutting out into the sea in front of what appears to be an isolated rocky islet (*Xecoftò*, i.e., the 'separate' place). The rocks are depicted close to a lip of light yellow sand (*Pachiamo*, i.e., course sand). Finally, the 'map' shows a long, broad, straw-coloured beach (*Sissamolacos*) interrupted at the eastern end by a small, isolated formation of rock that emerges from the water. We could not wait to see what this locality looked like in real life. The Venetians, who possessed the island from 1212 to 1669, called this place *Calus Limniones*: a promising, 'suggestive' Latin rendering of the Greek name, which in English might be translated as 'fair havens'.

Kalì Limenes is in fact situated in an enchanting bay with two long lips of sand. The beaches, where there are many eucalyptus and tamarisk trees, might be said to be in an enviable position if the scenery were not unfortunately marred by the presence of tall cylindrical cisterns that form part of a refuelling system located on the island of Pilos in front of the village. The first, fairly short beach (composed of light grey sand) in front of this small locality provides ample space for a number of caravans and campers; the second beach, to the west and bordered by two rocky walls, is quite wide and formed by light sand. We identified a third beach at the western end of the bay: this is definitely the most interesting, and is located in a relatively

*Kalì Liménes*

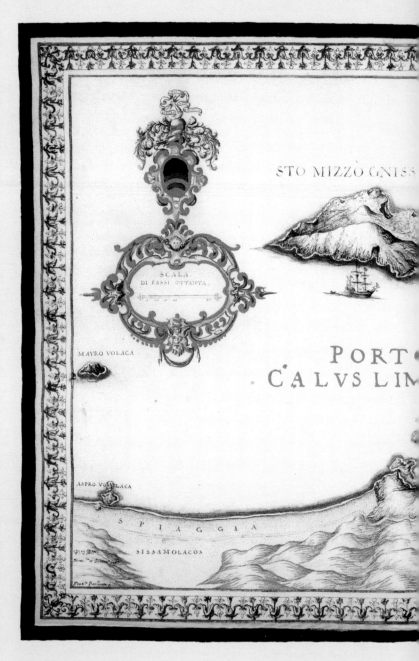

*Kalì Liménes.*
*Ancient print from Francesco Basilicata - Cretae Regnum 1618.*

MEGALO GNISSI.

STI CADEGLA

P<sup>TA</sup> DI S. NICOLÒ.

CANALE

STA STENA

DI
IONES

S. PIRNO
CHIERCATTI

PACHIAMO

*Chris òstomo*

secluded position beyond the low promontory at the top of which stands a solitary church (dedicated to Saint Paul the Apostle, who, according to tradition, landed here in the year 59 AD, on his journey to Rome). The beach is not marked but the Venetians called the small anchorage in front of it *Sta stenà*, which in Greek means 'narrow passage'. Only ten minutes away on foot, at first the site seems inaccessible as it is protected by a makeshift barrier of large branches that stops automobiles and visitors entering the area. Farther on, the beach is still cordoned off but we manage to get in by slipping through a large gap in the fence. After about one hundred yards, we reach an enchanting bay of dark sand and tiny pebbles. The beach is covered with smooth rocks (containing veins of white marble) that allow one to lie down close to the water's edge. At the sandbar, the seabed slopes down gradually into the sea for a few yards and then plummets to great depths and disappears into the dark water. The seaward landscape is far from monotonous, and the bay contains a small luxuriant rocky islet just a short distance from the shore, which divides it into two parts. To the right, there is a pretty natural harbour, where we notice a red and white boat moored to a tiny quay. To the left, a high wall of rock, which intersects another small island, impedes a direct view of the open sea. This time, we have the impression we are in a narrow Norwegian fjord (and we explore our fjord briefly, swimming in the crystal-clear water, which is still quite warm despite the time of year). The only blemish at this site was an old abandoned washing machine that someone decided might look good on the beach!

We go back to the coast road and from the higher ground we

*One of the beaches on the Kalì Limenes - Lendas route*

observe the sandy, 'well-equipped' beach at **Chrisòstomo**. This small tourist centre, which is predominantly formed by a group of holiday homes (some of which are still under construction), is separated from Kalì Limenes by a natural barrier of rock. Then, a few kilometres farther on, we find **Platià Peràmata**, a small harbour in front of a series of low farm buildings and greenhouses. From here on, we notice a string of small, deserted, nameless bays and inlets, some of which can be reached on foot and others from the sea. The conformation of the coastline is quite interesting and formed by fragile, greenish and pink, schistose rocks that dip steeply into the sea. To the north, the Liontaria, Tsouros and Vigla peaks of the Asteroussia range, which are in fact not extremely high, overlook the entire area. Before arriving in Lendas, we go down to the **Limanàki Beach**: a pebble-strewn strand at the end of a small, winding ravine, where we notice quite a few fishing boats. A few hundred yards father on, we see the dark sand and the leisure facilities at **Dytikòs**, an agricultural village full of greenhouses and magnificent bougainvillea, triumphantly adorning the gardens of the low summer houses.

**Lendas** is still the same small, quiet village we visited some years ago. The tavernas that serve fresh fish and let out rooms, the two small, sand and pebble beaches, the leisure facilities: nothing has changed at all and the place is never overcrowded. It is certainly worth stopping at Lendas, especially if one intends to visit the adjacent archaeological area, where the ancient city of Lébena once stood. The site, which is situated on ground a little way above the national highway, contains the remains of a Doric and Roman temple dedicated to

Asclepius that dates back to the third century BC. Visitors here will find a few mutilated columns, the large square slabs of an ancient altar and parts of a beautiful Roman mosaic depicting a sea-horse and two palm leaves. From the first century before the Common Era, the site was always famous for its thermal springs (they are actually still in use!) and was visited by pilgrims suffering from intestinal and digestive disorders. If from the high ground one looks out towards the Kefali promontory to the right, with a little imagination one can easily make out the shape of a squatting lioness (cf. the Phoenician word *lebena*), which appears to explain the origin of the ancient name of this place.

From Lendas, the road winds on beside the sea, passing through the solitary Paralìa Petraki and leading on to the Gulf of **Loutra.** Here, we find a small, protected anchorage surrounded by pinkish rock and fine pebbles and gravel. The little bay is located at the end of a ravine, where there is a taverna (also called 'Loutra'), and in the spacious inlet we notice excavators and dredging machinery digging into the beach: the workers inform us that a protected port is being built to facilitate the fishing activities in this area.

From this point, our itinerary turns inland and we drive up along the twisting road that leads to the villages of Kroto and Trìpti. We stop to take a last look at the splendid, long rugged coastline, with Kalì Limenes at the far western end and the long strands and bays that seem to end at the Kefali promontory, close to which there is a 'corrugated' rocky islet that resembles the shape of a seahorse. The panorama continues as far as the emerald and turquoise waters of the Libyan Sea at Loutra.

*Loutra*

# The beaches to the south of Spili

The village of Spili stands on a slope beneath Mount Kedros at an altitude of 600 m. It is worth visiting on account of its remarkable Venetian fountain, from which pure water constantly spills forth out of the mouths of thirty small lion heads. Filled with passing tourists during the day, the village has become an ideal base for groups of cyclists as the surrounding countryside offers many possibilities for pleasant excursions up into the mountains or down to the sea. The nearby beaches are very attractive on account of the landscape. The alternating mountainous areas and the little bays and inlets are off the main summer tourist routes and are peaceful and quiet. The shape of the two little islands of Paximadi a short distance from the shore can be seen all along this stretch of coastline.

Driving for about five kilometres along the road that connects Spili and Agia Galini, we pass by the village of Kissos on our right and then follow the direction indicated by the sign that points towards Keramés. We start to climb along an endless series of bends until we again catch glimpses of the sea. We drive through some remote, anonymous places, and after another twelve kilometres, reach Keramés, a village surrounded by hills and mountains. We follow the sign to **Ammoùdi** (cf. the Greek word *ammos*: 'sand'), located three kilometres farther on, and reach a point where the road ends in the middle of some fields. After crossing a makeshift bridge, we find ourselves in front of an unfinished stone and concrete construction, which projects out onto the sand and might be the newly-erected, inner framework of a future hotel or a large villa. Beside the deep-blue sea, the strand is formed by dark sand dunes and covered in scattered rocks and boulders.

Shortly afterwards, we reach **Agia Fotinì**, which is just a few kilometres away and clearly sign-posted. At this spot, there is a small mooring jetty, a stretch of course sand and a pretty taverna overlooking the sea. Stavros, the owner of this establishment (which offers four guest rooms), is a young Australian of Greek origin who inherited the business from his parents. Close to Stavros's taverna, the area in front of the harbour has been tastefully provided with amenities and deck chairs, and the effect is very pleasant. Out at sea, the Paximadi islets seem to act as sentinels that guard this magnificent, solitary place.

**Lìgres Beach** (7 km after Keramés) is also a pleasant spot. Here, you will find a long stretch of grey sand, two seafront tavernas and, at the eastern end, large prominent headlands overlooking the sea.

We drive on towards the east, where there are various other beaches and, amongst them, we feel that **Tris Petres** *('three rocks')*, which can be reached from Akoùmia by travelling along a very scenic, grit-surface road, is definitely the most charming of all. The locality owes its name to the presence of three enormous, flat though irregularly stratified  concretions, which form truncated pyramids and seem to be composed of rough, sculpted crystals. Tris Petres, which, on the landward side,  is protected by the Siderotas chain of mountains (some peaks are over 1,000 m high), has two immense beaches covered in very fine, dark pebbles. The place is probably full of visitors in the summer, but as there is so much space here it would probably not be difficult to find some peace and quiet; and anyone wishing to stay here can rent a room at one of the two tavernas. The only unsightly element is a large, seemingly incongruous, three-storey house which looms above the two low tavernas severely detracting from the charm of this site.

After Tris Petres, a partly-asphalted road leads on for another 3 km to **Agios Pavlos**. Around this small, delightful bay with lips of fine sand, the building development has been quite moderate. Walking towards the right, away from the small harbour and then along the beach, which is equipped with all the usual leisure facilities, a steep, wooden stairway leads up to the Melissa promontory, where the rock face sheer above the sea, eroded and shaped over thousands of years by the wind and the elements, has acquired spectacular forms. Metamorphic formations, which are highly concentrated in this part of the island, are the result of a long process of transformation caused by enormous pressure and high temperatures. The walk on the promontory is very interesting on account of the presence of the enormous slabs of rock with broad, black and white, horizontal strips that create a sort of 'optical-art' effect. From above, looking out on the southern side, we identify Tris Petres in the distance and **Dìplono Petres** immediately below us. The latter area, which has a few deck chairs and umbrellas, is an incredible stretch of sand (frequented mainly by nudists) that lies beside an almost vertical wall of sand dunes. It can be easily

reached if you follow the path that starts at the promontory.

Agios Pavlos can also be reached directly from Agia Galini. The small boat that leaves every morning at half past ten takes day-trippers also to **Agios Ioannis**, a tongue of dark sand which can also be accessed from the landward side by walking down the steps that start at Nikos' taverna.

**Agia Galini** is located 24 km after Spili. This beautiful village, formed by a nucleus of typical, white-washed houses built around the harbour in the 1800s, stands on a gentle slope beside the sea. At this village, which has a sandy beach that has become increasingly crowded in recent years, it is perhaps only the opportunity of going on boat trips to the nearby inlets that induces people to prolong their stay.

Again, following the coast road, we reach **Kòkkino Pìrgos**, a harbour village with a small beach of sand and pebbles, and then, a few kilometres farther on, **Kalamàki**, with its long strands that border on the archaeological site of **Kommòs**, which has been identified as one of the ancient ports of Festòs. On the northern side, Kommòs offers a beach shaded by tamerisk trees, which has been partially fenced off to protect the loggerhead turtles that stop here to lay and hatch their eggs. The southern side is where you will find the excavations.

*Dìplono Petres*

# The beaches from Préveli to Frangokàstello

Préveli is famous for its natural beauty. Here, you will find a turquoise-coloured sea and fine, light sand set against a backdrop of palm trees and oleander around a narrow embayment in front of the Kurtalioti gorge. Although now one of the most popular resorts in Crete, it remains a tiny paradise: especially if you visit the place in the first week of May, as we did, without the hordes of tourists.

To reach Préveli just follow the signs to the historic monastery of Monì Préveli. You will go along a narrow, winding road that leads through the sharp peaks of the Kurtalioti ravine almost right up to the monastery itself. From there, a road to the left leads down to the beach and a car-park. To be honest, in past years the presence of the parking lot (which is not free) had made us rather diffident: in our case it acted as a great dissuader and on seeing it we were put off. This time however, looking down from above to view the area, it takes us no more than a second to realise what a splendid this place is and we decide to give it a try. Leaving our car in the custody of the parking attendant for the modest sum of 1.5 euro, we walk down the steps that lead to **Préveli Beach**. This pleasant, 15-min walk down the footpath, amongst bright-yellow, threadlike esparto grass and the intense golden colour of Jerusalem Sage (*phlomis fruticosa*), reveals an enchanting scene. There in front of us, we see a long stretch of dark sand protected on the landward side by tamerisk trees, canebrakes, tall palms and eucalyptus trees. The sea seems to flow into the ravine and penetrate the almost tropical vegetation but it really simply forms a tiny lagoon, which is excellent for swimming (and can be explored with pedal boats). The river that descends from the gorge, the Megalo Potami, divides the beach into two halves, obliging us to wade through a narrow stream of water. The tiny bar has not opened yet and the beach has not been covered with umbrellas and deck chairs: we think of all this wonderful solitude as a kind of privilege. It is also a really marvellous experience to swim peacefully in such crystal-clear water, with waves that were little more than gentle ripples.

We go back towards Monì Préveli and after a few kilometres reach Lefkògia. From here, we descend towards the Gulf of Damnòni, which has a few interesting beaches. The first is at **Ammoudi.** We leave the main road to follow a sign on the left that points towards the Ammoùdi Hotel and reach the village after less than one kilometre. Solitary and tranquil, the beach, composed of light sand and fine white pebbles is located in an inlet sheltered by rocks and provided with shade by the tamerisk trees. The beach in the **Damnòni bay**, composed of sand and small boulders, also seems very pleasant but we notice to our dismay that an enormous tourist complex is being constructed there. The bungalows, tennis courts and swimming-pools will soon detract from the tranquillity of the place.

Immediately afterwards, we arrive at **Plakìas**, an expanding resort in a broad inlet with a long, wide beach. It is far too crowded and full of hotels, so we decide to go back up to the main road. On this very scenic route, we pass through Sellià and then reach Rodàkino. From this pretty, 'authentic' village we descend again for about two kilometres towards **Koràka**, where there are three beaches. The first is vast and welcoming, the second quite small, and the third beach, below the Kastellos (Akrotiri Kastellos) promontory, is quite narrow. Close to the latter we find a taverna and some bungalows beside a large open courtyard, which, in this rural context, looks like a farmyard. Quite by chance, near Koràka, we came across a delightful **hidden inlet,** located beyond the promontory. We get there by following the signs that indicate the Hotel Polyrizo and then turn left towards the Orizon taverna. We then walk along a path (10 mins) that leads down to the Libyan Sea, through fields of barley, olive groves, citrus fruit orchards and large oleander trees that grow spontaneously over the now dried-up bed of a small stream. The beach, composed of fine sand and small pebbles, is lonely and deserted and 'crowned' by high rocks, where it is possible to find shelter. On the landward side, the massive Mt. Krioneritis stands out in a rather bucolic panorama._

Leaving the Province of Réthymnon, the highway winds on above the coast and enters the Sphakià area: the 'wildest' territory in Crete. We know we have entered this area when begin to catch glimpses of its high mountains, the names of which (Atsalokefala, Agriokefala, Perissinaki, Dafnolakki) seem to have a slightly 'aggressive' sound. After Argoulés and Skalotì, our favourite beach in this area is the one beneath the imposing, sepia-coloured walls of the mysterious mediaeval castle at **Frangokàstello**, which, with its silent towers, protrudes outwards towards the sea.

The castle, the original structure of which is very well preserved, was built in the mid-14th century and renovated in 1594 by the Venetian *Provveditore* Nicolò Donà. A few years later, it  was finally abandoned, and the citizens of Sphakia even removed the *"travadure alle torri e alle stanze"* [wooden beams of the rooms and turrets]. In this case, the Italian name Castelfranco means 'Castle of the Franks', but many centuries ago, the Cretans might have used the term 'Frankish' to refer to the Franks, the Venetians and all foreigners in general. The castle stands by a vast stretch of fine sand, where you will find deck chairs, large beach umbrellas and a small taverna close to a group of tamarisks. Over to the right, there is also, unfortunately, a construction which has been left unfinished. It is not the first time we decide to spend a few hours at this enchanted spot in the hours just before sunset: at this time of day Frangokàstello becomes cloaked in a very special, almost magical atmosphere. The beach, above which looms a picturesque lighthouse, is crowded: but only with tourists that have come to spend a day here. It is ideal for children, as the sandbar slopes gently into the sea and the water is a little warmer here with respect to the other beaches on the island. Close by, there are two churches: Agios Nikìta, built on the ruins of an early Christian basilica and decorated with an interesting mosaic paving in the front courtyard, and Agios Caralambos. According to an old tradition, at dawn on the 18th of May, a ghost army composed of *droussolites* (the 'men of the morning dew') materialises out of thin air. The apparitions were once believed to be the spirits of Sphakian warriors, returning to parade along the battlements of the castle. A group of soldiers led by Chatzimichalis Daliànis was in fact massacred by the Turks in 1828 at a nearby site. A more scientific explanation suggests that the optical illusion is a 'Fata Morgana' mirage, which can be experienced under certain ideal weather conditions; when there is no wind and a calm sea, the images of soldiers training on the nearby Libyan coast may be actually reflected here. In any case, on that very day, the suggestive legend does attract a lot of people.

*Frangokàstello*

# The northern beaches: from Màlia to Réthymnon

Along the northern coastline of Crete, between Màlia and Heràklion in the west, there is an almost uninterrupted succession of long golden strands. However, many of the beaches, and in particular those located close to large hotels and modern holiday complexes - as occurs in the villages of Stalìda, Hersònissos, Goùves and Goùrnes - have been spoilt by the frantic urge to develop the tourist trade. An exception that would confirm the general rule is the broad beach at **Amnisos** close to Heràklion airport. This sandy strand located in front of the rocky offshore islet of Dias is fully equipped with deck chairs and beach umbrellas but seems reasonably quiet. We decide to pass by the 'city beaches' of Heràklion and drive on westwards, where in two broad inlets we find Lygarià and Agia Pelagìa.

**Lygarià**, a village enclosed within a natural, rocky inlet surrounded by high cliffs, does not look like a typical tourist resort at all; but it does give one the impression that the people of Heràklion at least, many of whom have built impressive villas here, have chosen this spot as their ideal getaway.

The bay after Lygarià is **Agia Pelagìa**. In the year 1412, in his *Descriptio Insulae Candiae,* Cristoforo Buondelmonti mentions the beach located at this site and states that along the shore he had seen a crowd of sick people standing with their legs buried in the sand: an ancient ritual which apparently had the purpose of preventing diseases involving the limbs. The modern Agia Pelagìa is filled with tavernas and bars and has a rather narrow, constantly crowded beach.

We continue to follow the broad, winding coast road that offers us glimpses of the sea and then suddenly turns inland. We pass by **Fòdele Beach**, which is just a little too close to a tourist complex of brightly-coloured, one-storey houses, and then, at a point about 40 km outside the capital (close to Sìses) we pass through some orange groves

*Prèveli beach*

to reach the two beaches of **Aliki** and **Almyrida** just off the national highway. Aliki is in a spacious inlet, where there are some old ruined houses and quite singularly shaped rocks that soar like pinnacles above the sea. At Almyrida, which is also located in a small sandy inlet, there is a small harbour, some rather humble-looking holiday homes and a small bar, close to olive groves, canebrakes and a few vegetable plots.

Five kilometres after Almyrida, from the road we notice a group of caravans and camping vehicles parked close to the shore. We pass through a gateway, next to a very visible sign that warns visitors of the presence of roaming flocks of sheep, and walk onto a pebble beach. We notice that it would be quite difficult to go swimming here as the rocks are very sharp and pointed.

We continue along the winding road and finally get to **Balì.** This pretty village is spread out over three small headlands and around three splendid inlets, which do tend to get very crowded in the summertime. **Pànormo** (9 km farther on) is also a pleasant locality worth visiting. In this small village, where an ancient castle stands perched on a rocky spur overlooking a small sandy beach, we notice that many old stone dwelling houses have been restored so as to preserve their original features,.

After Pànormo, below the Geropotamos bridge, we find another broad sandy beach, a part of which is used by the nearby Hotel Panorama. The strand can also be reached by walking along a rough grit road that also passes under the bridge.

From here, the road to Réthymnon passes by long stretches of sand - some totally 'free' and others equipped with various tourist amenities and facilities - in the proximity of Stravoménos, Sfakaki, Adelianòs Kàmpos and Plataniàs. Just outside Réthymnon the beaches are generally monopolised by the 5-star hotels. In Réthymnon itself, where visitors will certainly notice a lingering Venetian atmosphere, a long beach located just beyond the old harbour is intensely exploited by tourists.

We prefer not to stop in the city and continue our exploration of the coastline, travelling on towards Episkopì. In this area, the 9-km stretch of coastline frequented by bathers stretches as far as **Georgioùpolis,** an interesting town built on the banks of a river, the centre of which is reached by driving along a shady avenue of enormous eucalyptus trees. The beach here is composed of very fine, almost powdery sand, but the sea has very strong currents. If you have children, you will have to be careful.

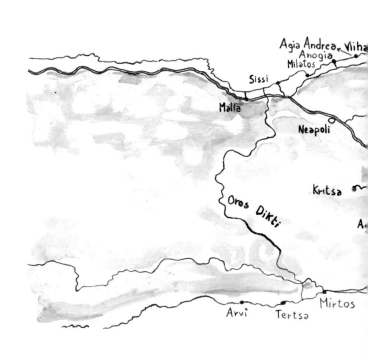

# Eastern Crete

Georgios
Ag. Ioannis
Plaka
Kolokithia
Elounda

Akri Tenta
Erimoupolis
Vai
Maridati
Kouremenos
Chiona

Sitia
Palekastro

ios Nicolaos
miros          Tholos
voulisma Istron
Karavoustasi

Hohlakies
Farangi

Ori Sitias

Zakros

Kato Zakros

leiman
Pachia Ammos

Ziros

Xerokambos

Galini
Makrigialos
Ag. Fotiá        Moní Kapsa
etra

Ag. Irini

Goudouras Gulf

Erimoùpoli

Kolokitha

# The beaches at Elounda

We perhaps risk being impartial when we speak about Elounda. We have lived in this area for many years and every time we return here, after spending a few months somewhere else, we cannot resist stopping for a while up on the high belvedere a few kilometres after Agios Nikòlaos to enjoy the expansive view of the bay: the magnificent panorama always fills us with joy. Our vision even becomes 'selective', and we tend to ignore the 5-star tourist structures that clutter up an extensive portion of the coastline and just absorb the beauty of the isthmus, the vast island of Kolokìtha and the silhouette of the fortress on the island of Spinalonga. Elounda was the setting of the successful English television series *Who pays the ferryman?* and perhaps it has retained some of that glory. The town does perhaps have a claim to fame, but we think it really lives up to it only in the part around its pretty harbour.

After **Elounda**, ignoring those stretches of sand now exploited by the luxury hotels, **Kolokìtha** beach is undoubtedly the most attractive. The strand is in a magnificent inlet, in which, centuries ago, the quay offered mooring space for up to fifty warships, or so we are told by Francesco Basilicata in a report sent to the Venetian Senate in 1630.

Kolokìtha can be reached by sea or by land. Those who come here by sea are generally excursionists, dropped off at the beach by the ferryboats that monopolise it from eleven o'clock in the morning until five in the afternoon, discharging onto the sand hundreds of tourists attracted by the prospect of their 'all-in' day trip (which will invariably include an hour-long visit to the Spinalonga fortress and then the ritual barbecue event on the beach). However, as if by magic, Kolokìtha regains all of its splendour in the late afternoon, and if you are in the area it is certainly worth visiting the spot for a few hours. Again, starting from Elounda, just before the picturesque harbour, you will find a sign that points in the direction of the ruins of Olous. On days when the tide ebbs to its lowest level, the submerged ruins of this ancient city of the Hellenistic period in fact become visible by the side of the long, slender isthmus, on one side of which there are the former Venetian salt works, and, on the other, the remains of some powerful old windmills. After passing by a small bridge, you may wish to follow the signs that lead to the small Agios Loukas church. Continue now along the scenic, grit road until you reach an open space where there is a recently-restored chapel. Leave your car here and follow the descending footpath which will take you through some typical Mediterranean *maquis*. This is where you will enter the Kolokìtha peninsula. Shall we call it a natural botanical garden? In the springtime it is blanketed with violet anemones, light purple buttercups and vast populations of fuchsia-coloured gladioli; at the end of summer, white, perfumed lilies appear on the sand; and, later on, in winter, in the lower patches and dips, you will notice the delicate narcissus. It is a delightful experience to go swimming in this tiny bay. You will find powdery sand, crystal clear waters, and the gradient of the seabed beyond the sandbar is such that you need not worry about suddenly slipping into deep water. The gradually enveloping peacefulness of the evening, when the strand is silently visited by fishermen and late divers, always seems to generate a desire to stay on as long as possible at this spot.

Following the coast road as far as **Plaka**, after Elounda there are various other small inlets with sand and pebbles. Plaka was once a quiet hamlet with a few modest houses built around the quay but has now become yet another innocent prey to the frenetic and seemingly inexorable proliferation of tourist structures. Just outside the little village you will find a wide beach, with large pearl-grey pebbles smoothed by the continuous backwash of water. The strand is bordered by tamerisk trees and filled with deck chairs during the summer months. In our opinion, the water here is the most transparent in the whole area. From this point, there is also a splendid view of the island fortress of Spinalonga, which can be reached in five minutes by boat.

From Plaka, we would suggest you now go out to the Agios Ioannis promontory for a trip to the lighthouse. Take the road that leads to Vrouhàs; before the village, a small now-faded and almost illegible sign on the right indicates the aeolian park and the small church (Agios Ioannis). On the promontory, one feels almost crushed by the presence of the powerful blades of these modern windmills, which emit a deafening roar. They seem to be engaged in a titanic struggle with the wind, which always blows hard at this site. Leaving our vehicle in front of the church, we start off on foot along the path that leads to the small inlet of **Agios Ioannis** and then on to the lighthouse.

*Agios Ioannis*

Until just a few years ago, this would have been quite an adventurous excursion: from the Agios Ioannis chapel, only a steep, rough track led down to the sea; and along the way, there was the constant risk of slipping on the rocks and ending up a cropper in the thorny euphorbia bushes. For some reason, the pathway has now been transformed into a wide dirt road: not yet passable, but which easily leads down to the lower ground. It goes as far as a ridge, where you will be able to see a small anchorage. Although nothing has spoilt the splendid panorama ranging all across from the open Cretan Sea to the Gulf of Mirabello on the two sides of the Agios Ioannis promontory, the former 'wild' charm of the excursion has been lost forever.

On reaching flat ground, to get to the inlet, which is below us and to the right, one has to clamber very carefully over a number of large boulders. This small bay, protected from the winds, gave us moments of real joy: the water is crystal clear, and, depending on depth, has shades that range from a very light blue to a greenish turquoise and very deep blue. Here, the solitude is 'absolute solitude', interrupted occasionally by a few passing fishing boats that sometimes come this far (as is confirmed by the old pieces of net, traces of bait and hooks we find abandoned on the shore.

After having our fill of the sea, we stop to rest a while and then continue - very cautiously - along a narrow mule-track sheer above the sea that leads on to the lighthouse: a 'powerful' construction, most of which is in ruins. We are told that at night its light can be seen very clearly by the passengers on the ferryboat that sails from the Piraeus to the port of Agios Nikolaos; though the days when a lighthouse keeper lived here all year round are long gone: the building is now deserted. There is nothing else to do here, so we double back around the cape towards the point we started from. Amongst the scanty vegetation at this site, the euphorbia bushes, wild thyme and juniper (*iuniperus phoenicea*) seem to have been 'stretched' and elongated by the wind, and flattened against the ground in curious forms.

If you go on this walk in midsummer, it is best to start either very early in the morning or in the late afternoon. We have memories of an unforgettable flame-filled sky we once saw in July as the sun was setting over the sea. The air was very cool and the windmills cast their early evening shadows along the crest of the hill.

The descent is not exceptionally difficult, however it is advisable to wear gym shoes or light hiking boots. This is also quite a good spot for a picnic, so why not take some food and drinks? An hour and a half would be sufficient for this excursion.

Vlihàdia

# The northern beaches

From Elounda we travel up along the northern coast. After Vrouhàs, the road begins to wind up through olive groves and plantations and, one after the other, we drive through the rather neglected villages of Sélles, Loùmas and Skiniàs. These little places seem inhabited exclusively by senior citizens: we notice many old women dressed in black, wiling away their time, embroidering or sewing on the thresholds of their humble homes, and the old men sitting around tables at the *kafeneion,* indulging perhaps in one of the Cretans' favourite pastimes: lengthy discussions about politics. At Skiniàs we follow the sign that points in the direction of Vlihàdia and go down a winding road as far as the *kritikò pelagos* (the Cretan Sea). Vlihàdia seems to have known better days. There are a few greenhouses, a vaguely-designed landing jetty and just one taverna. Keep to the left, and park close to the typical, old one-storey house, and then look out across the sea far below. There is a wonderful little bay close by with a gravel and pebble beach that can be reached on foot by descending a recently-constructed, stone stairway. You will also see that the nearby inlet comprises a dried-up river-bed located between two high walls of rock, which is home for an entire population of small birds. The cavities at the bottom of the cliff faces moreover provide their own form of shelter and make up for the lack of trees. Those who love to sunbathe and get a rich suntan, can also stretch out on the smooth, white slabs of rock, freshened by the sea spray sent up by the crashing waves below. To appreciate **Vlihàdia** to the full however, we suggest you pay attention to winds blowing in from the sea: the place is ideal for bathing only when the sea is calm and the breeze is not too strong. One curious thing we noticed is that the presence of quite a few elderly folk: if you arrive about mid-morning, you will often come across these 'older' bathers, who slowly wend their way down from their little houses on the promontory above, aided by walking sticks and protected by broad-rimmed straw hats, to go and sit close to the shore. They seem to enjoy stopping close to the water to gaze out at the horizon, and then calmly go in for a swim. Once in the water, they appear to acquire as if by magic the lost agility of their youth. We have seen quite a few octogenarians, otherwise slightly unstable on their feet, happily pirouetting in the water and adventurous grandmothers, perhaps accompanied by their grandchildren, who go out for a swim in their one-piece costumes (and black, of course, would generally be *de rigueur*) They often stroll around, sporting parasols, and peacefully indulge in long conversations with old friends. This is the way it should be. For these people, the sea becomes a source of joy and great pleasure: it offers an opportunity to practise beneficial, healthy pastimes and, at the same time, stimulates social activity.

If you intend to explore this area a little further, another interesting site you may wish to visit is the inlet close to **St. Andrew's Hermitage**, with a small beach (good for bathing) a short distance away from a monastery. The point of departure is the village of Finokalià, about 20 km from Elounda. When we visited this typical Cretan village of small whitewashed houses, an old lady helped us find the monastery (we felt her generosity was perhaps partly driven by a desire to have someone to talk to). Just outside the village, to the right, the site is clearly indicated by a sign. The long, paved, concrete road that leads out to the monastery is rather narrow. In a few parts, it is even overgrown by encroaching shrubs of Greek Sage (*salvia fruticosa*), with its trilobite, velvety-textured leaves, light violet flowers, and Giant Fennel (*ferula communis)*, an herbaceous plant rich with a yellow, tightly-bunched inflorescence. Giant Fennel is a plant that was mentioned by Hesiod, who wrote how Prometheus had transported the fire he had stolen from the

*Near Agios Andreas*

Gods in one of these plants. The dry medulla of the flowers is also still used as wick material as it burns very slowly and can be easily carried about when lit. Four kilometres farther on, we find the now-abandoned monastery, sheltered by a gorge. The surviving parts are the ancient church (wedged in the rock face) and, just in front of it, a recent construction, which is probably used as a guest house on the saint's day. Saint Andrew's church has been fully restored. It appears that the only original aperture is the tiny one in the outer, western wall, now an aedicule window with a pediment and two small, graceful columns. The inside is carved out of the rock, except for the altar area, which is surrounded by an attractive, wooden iconostasis altar screen with inlay work and old icons that have become blackened with age and candle smoke.

Beyond the church, the road degenerates into a grit-surface road. Continuing along the track, you will pass by a dense thicket of cluster pines on the right and then approach a large open space, from which you will be able to continue on foot along a steep footpath. Along the way, we come across an old fountain, from which, despite its now ruined state, a generous quantity of water still gushes forth. All around, artificial terracing and grape vines now growing wild suggest the place was only recently abandoned. After walking  through a narrow passageway  carved out of the rock between some large boulders, we emerge at the edge of a small rocky anchorage. This wild site is 'protected' on the landward side by a high, reddish wall of alluvial soil looming above the beach. The only visitors to this place are a few divers, who, armed with spear-guns, go off looking for fish in the open sea. We gradually enter the water, stepping down over patches of gravel into crystal clear water, diagonally streaked by a deep, large vein of sand which turns the water a light blue colour. We have visited this inlet at two different times of year: the first was at the end of March, when the temperature was not quite right for bathing, and then in late September, when we were really able to enjoy the sea. In the spring, this enchanting place is definitely interesting also from the botanical point of view as the countryside near the coast is not as arid as practically everywhere else on the island. The terrain is covered in a rich vegetation, which can only be explained by the presence of water that filters down from higher ground through the narrow gorge. Rarely have we seen concentrated in one area so many flowers and wild shrubs: Cretan Birthwort (*aristolochia cretica*), curved, U-shaped flowers with a dark purple colour; the delicate Small Restharrow (*ononis reclinata*), a low shrub with downy leaves and flowers with a pinkish corolla; yellow anemones and red buttercups; and the pale-gold, Yellow Kidney-Vetch (*anthyllis hermanniae)*. This pleasant excursion becomes slightly difficult only on the track leading down to the sea, where it is best to wear hiking boots or gym shoes. If you intend to spend the whole day here, then it is best to prepare sandwiches and take some water.

Starting off again from Finokalià, before going to the beach at **Anògia,** we used this opportunity to explore the wilder area of the northern part of the island, passing through various villages located high up in hills, such as Nofaliàs, which overlooks the sea in the distance, or remote places in the midst of olive plantations and vineyards, such as Kouroùnes, from where a pleasant but rough road leads down into the valleys below. On this trip we discovered an abandoned monastery complex in a glade of tall cypresses known as *Xerà Xìlia*, which means 'dry wood', and majestic ancient ruins called *'palea spiti'*. This was perhaps one of the fortress homes that the Venetians built in the fertile countryside of the eastern part of Crete. We then reached the silent villages of Agios Antonios and Anògia. When you pass through Anògia, you will see a sign that points towards the beach (*paralia*), which is 4 km along a dirt road that descends in a zig-zag fashion over a vast, barren promontory covered in bramble bushes. At the end of summer the headland is made a little prettier by tall white sheaves of sea squill (*urginea marittima*). Close to the sea we find a few modest houses here and there: probably restructured cottages at one time inhabited by the shepherds, who would bring their families and their flocks down to this milder climate, far from the harsher conditions of the highlands. A little farther away, we see that some imaginative individual has transformed an old abandoned coach into a seaside holiday home, with sheet-metal walls and a vegetable patch in front.

The Anogia coastline is in fact a vast bay with various solitary inlets. It faces east, in the direction of Mìlatos and the tourist resorts of Màlia and Hersònissos. From here one can also see in the distance the rocky islet of Dìa. One particular inlet seemed quite beautiful: in a central position with respect to the others, it is noticeable by the presence of its one and only tamerisk tree. The beach is a long strip of white gravel with rocks emerging from the sea. During our initial investigation of this area

*Anogia*

we did not notice this small inlet because one has to look down from above to be able to see it. In any case, it can be reached either by sea or by walking down over the rocks, following a rather difficult route that runs along the bed of a dried-up stream. Farther west, another inlet with a beach composed of pebbles and boulders (not so difficult to get to, and offering more tamerisk trees) offers easy access to the sea.

From Anògia it is possible to drive up into the hills to Mìlatos, where the villagers all seem to share the same ambition of restructuring their old dwelling houses in the traditional way, using dark stone from the surrounding countryside. However, there's a different tale to be told and a different atmosphere down at **Paralia Mìlatos,** the beach close to the village of Mìlatos, which is just one kilometre away. Here, there are tavernas that offer good seafood dishes, a small beach (not very useful, on account of the position of the rocks) and a delightful little harbour, which is already showing a few signs of hurried development projects to boost the tourist trade and the "let's do it quick" approach.

Still following the coast, a few kilometres farther on you will find Sissi. This is a very pleasant village with a small harbour, which was created in a narrow inlet (similar to a fjord) that projects inwards deeply on the landward side. The western side is covered with luxuriant, pleasantly exotic vegetation, with tamerisk trees growing close to some palm trees. To the north, you will notice the imposing mass of Mount Selene, which stands out in the 'backdrop' scenery provided by the Lassithi mountain chain. **Sissi Beach** is just outside the village to the east: this is a small, tranquil bay located at the end of a water course, the high banks of which become rockier as they get closer to the sea and fortunately hide from view a large tourist complex on the right. The beach is wide, covered with fine, light-coloured sand and is equipped with various amenities, including beach umbrellas, deck chairs and a small bar.

*Sissi*

# The beaches in the Gulf of Mirabello

**Agios Nikòlaos**, located in the north-eastern part of the island, faces the Gulf of Mirabello: an Italian name which in itself suggests natural beauty. There are many beaches along this vast embayment (Almiròs, Ammoudàra, Ammoùdi) and their sand gradually gives way to the fine gravel and pebbles of the typical city beach of **Kitroplatìa** (translated literally, the Greek name means 'the cedar square'). Centuries ago, citrus fruits were stored and shipped at this point, which, being in the heart of the city, was easy to reach. At this beach, now a traditional meeting place for local people, you will find all the usual beach amenities.

If you walk from the town towards the mini golf-course and the other sports facilities, in a quarter of an hour you will reach one of the local beaches we know quite well and often visit: **Almiròs**. We have many reasons for liking this strand: there is a stream that flows through the cane-brakes behind it; we enjoy the impressive backdrop of the Thripti mountains; the place is very quiet; Dimitri the lifeguard, who is also in charge of hiring out deck chairs and umbrellas, is a very friendly sort of person; the seabed slopes away very gently from the shallow sandbar; and there is a small taverna-bar that offers samples of Cretan cuisine.

Nor will you ever get bored at Almiròs: with all that space, you can play beach volleyball; there is a small playground for little children and a wooden bridge over the river (where you can observe sea turtles and large black mullet swimming in the very cold water); or you could try one of the water sports. From June to October, the beach attracts large numbers of local people (especially on Saturdays and Sundays), but you never find the crowds you see on southern European beaches during the summer. In particular, there is never much noise: the only music allowed here is that produced by the waves breaking on the shore.

Following the coast road towards Sitìa, after Almiròs you will find **Ammoudàra**, another strand with leisure facilities and a few tavernas

*Almiròs*

that serve the excellent seafood dishes the local people enjoy. The road then turns inland and passes through low hills covered in olive plantations. Here, you will find Kalò Choriò and the **Karavostàsi beach**: a long strip of sand that continues eastwards and suddenly changes its name to **Agios Pantelèimon** (here, the beach is named after the old, whitewashed church at the far end). Agios Pantelèimon (also known as the 'Silver Beach') is 'crowned' with a strip of tamerisk trees, olive trees, canebrakes and even vegetable gardens. At the far left end of Karavostàsi, a short dirt road leads to two interesting inlets: the first beside a stone house with pretty, blue window frames, and the second set back a short distance and more secluded, immersed in an area covered in low cluster pines and rockrose.

You will find the Voùlisma beach (aka the '**Golden Beach'**) 18 km after Agios Nikòlaos in the direction of Sitìa, just outside the village of Istron. The second name 'Golden Beach' is more apt on account of the fine light-coloured sand that borders this broad inlet with a long central strand and some pretty embayments with leisure facilities, deck chairs and umbrellas. During our first years on the island of Crete we often went to Voùlisma, as we were enchanted by the turquoise sea and the gently sloping sandbar, which makes swimming easier and is great for very young children. In May and June we experienced the tranquillity of this wonderful site, and in July and August saw all the crowds. In the summer months, we came across so many of our compatriots speaking Italian; the infernal 'water motorbikes' would be dashing  about across the water, and the happy screams and shouting of the fearless passengers on the 'banana boats' could be heard everywhere. We did appreciate however the scrupulous work of the beach-cleaning brigade: their work is always impeccable. They take great care over 'combing' the shore every morning with a sort of enormous brush that removes everything that is swept up when the scirocco is blowing. All in all, this is an ideal beach for families or groups of excursionists. There is also a small kiosk at the end of the beach that serves simple snacks and drinks, and you will find various tavernas along the coastal road above.

After Istron, the newly-constructed section of the coast road will let you drive on very quickly towards the eastern part of the island. Travelling east, you will also pass the archaeological site at Gurnià, which is situated on a low hill just a few yards from the sea. The site - an important example of a trading port of the Minoan age - contains a labyrinth of winding streets (once lined with tiny shops), which led up to the agorà and acropolis on the high ground.

You may then wish to visit the long beach at Pachìa Ammos, the Greek name of which means 'course sand'. Unfortunately, along this stretch of coast, the currents almost constantly wash up considerable quantities of rubbish onto the shore. Its saving grace is the presence of a few very good tavernas specialised in fresh seafood dishes and tasty Cretan *mezés*. These typical Cretan *hors d'oeuvres* include such specialities as rice-filled vine leaves, fried pasta balls made of cheese and vegetables, creamy yogurt sauces, egg-plant dishes and 'sea eggs' (*taramàs*). We must refrain from getting sidetracked: if we were to illustrate the fabulous gastronomic attractions of the island, the list would go on forever.

After Pachìa Ammos, there are two possibilities: straight on towards Ieràpetra or the magnificent coast road to Sitìa. We opt for the second route as we have not yet visited the beach at **Thòlos** (under the jurisdiction of the nearby village of Kavoùssi), which is not very wide and occasionally hit by the strong currents mentioned earlier. We should also like to advise our readers to stop off at Sfàka, from where, **Mòhlos** is only a 10-km drive away. Enchanting in all seasons, this village is in a small bay, where you will find a tiny beach. The harbour at Mòhlos seems to be a favourite spot for the inhabitants of Agios Nikòlaos and Sitìa, who tend to come here a lot at weekends: presumably, on account of its secluded position, the romantic atmosphere along the shore and of course the small restaurants that always serve very good food. You may also be interested in visiting the rocky holm just in front of Mòhlos. If the wind is not too strong, and you are too impatient to wait for the ferry, you might consider swimming the 150 yards across to this rocky islet. On the island you can visit fascinating Minoan tombs that once contained jewellery now preserved at the Archaeological Museum in Heràklion.

**Sitìa** is located 40 km after Mòhlos. You will find this is a quiet little town, far from the exasperating crowds of tourists that invade the northern part of the island every year. Dominated by the *Kazarma*, an ancient Turkish fortress built on the ruins of a Venetian castle, Sitìa offers a tranquil urban atmosphere around a pleasant seafront lined with tavernas and bars.

*Mòhlos*

# The beaches near Sitìa on the eastern coast

Our exploration of the eastern coast was an enchanting experience. The area, which is divided by a watershed at Palékastro, presents a succession of rocky promontories and small sandy inlets, long solitary strands, gorges that lead down to the sea and famous beaches such as the palm forest at Vài.

We leave Sitìa and drive along the winding road that leads up to the 15<sup>th</sup>-century monastery of Toploù. This ancient building can be recognised from some way off by the shape of its Latin bell tower, which suddenly appears after kilometres of low hills and barren mountainsides. This part of the island is still rather remote, however we have heard that the vast area surrounding this old convent is to be soon exploited within the framework of a 'valorisation' project. In other words, they are talking about a 'tourist trade' project; and 'valorisation' implies the creation of golf courses and holiday residences. Let's hope it doesn't happen too soon!

This solitary landscape is still very charming. In summer it is inhabited by the goats and in the wintertime covered by large roaming flocks of sheep that occasionally cross roads and stop the traffic as they lazily migrate from one field to another. When it happens, the expressions of these curious animals seem to reveal a kind of incredulity on their part: how dare we disturb them in their own habitat? The territory is very dry and barren, and typically presents large patches of a variety of spurge (*euforbia acantothamnos*): thorny, aromatic shrublets with a generally rounded, compact and intricate ramification.

After Toploù we reach the junction where it is possible to turn off towards the **Vài** palm forest. We ignore the signs that point in the direction of this beach. Vài is very famous on account of its beauty and

*Vai*

a long, sandy strand equipped with all the leisure facilities, but it has now been exploited to such a degree that it has lost most of its undeniable exotic charm. We go on towards **Erimoùpoli** and reach the ancient Minoan city of Itanos, which is spread around a rocky promontory with splendid inlets at the sides. One of these, to the right of the archaeological site, is crowned by a tiny forest of tall palm trees and bordered with very fine sand and patches of tall, slender beach grass (*ammophila arenaria*). How did the palm trees get there? According to tradition, the date palms (*phoenix Theophrastii*) were 'imported' by the Saracen troops of Abu Haab, who camped here in 825 AD and sacked and destroyed the ancient city.

There is another beach on the opposite, left-hand side of the headland, which can be reached on foot. To do so, just follow the track (above, and to the right) that winds between some jagged green and violet-tinged rock formations. After about ten minutes you will walk out onto a strand of clear, light sand (with no amenities) that slopes down into turquoise water.

Itanos is the ideal place for anyone who wants to combine their archaeological interests with a visit to the sea: the remains of the ancient city can be found spread out across two hills of the promontory, with the acropolis at the summit. We felt the site is however inadequately protected against negligent bathers and visitors. The entire area is known as **Erimoùpoli,** and at the time of our visit in the middle of August we paused only for a brief rest in the bay. We have a vivid memory of a picture post-card scene with a white and blue boat and a small hut covered in tree branches, where *souvlaki* (roast meat on skewers) and drinks are served to the tourists. The site is generally frequented by people from the nearby towns and villages but also from much farther afield. Seeking greater solitude, we then went on along the road that winds up towards Cape Sìdero, the easternmost tip of the island. From high up, one enjoys a really 'expansive' view. Towards the east, there is a succession of rocky headland formations and inlets all along the indented coastline and stretches of sand that continue as far as the Kastri promontory. The monotony of the open sea is also made more interesting by the small Elàssa islet in front of Itanos and then the Grandes rock, close to Palékastro.

We then continue along this road until we find a very visible warning sign that forbids entry to the military zone in front of us, which forms part of a Greek Navy base, but at this point we have reached our destination. The **Gulf of Tenta** and its crystal-clear, turquoise waters appear before us on the right in a magnificent bay characterised by a series of flat slabs of rock.

The small gulf presents a series of small, natural embayments. We find one of them particularly charming: a small inlet bordered by very

Cape Sidero

Koureménos

light sand, which forms a natural, semi-circular swimming-pool. The inviting water is a very light blue, which then turns into a more intense, deeper blue as the water gets deeper. If you are quite good at swimming or diving, keep to the right-hand side, beneath the high walls of rock, and after about fifty yards you will find a series of grottoes (about ten all in all) that conceal an iridescent aquarium. In one of these caverns, which are very spacious, the dark inner cavity is suddenly brightened by a perfectly round beam of light that reveals the presence of a siphon which swimmers can easily pass through. The water here is full of marine organisms and small, colourful fish: curious tiny shrimps that will swarm against your diving mask, large, light pink, coral red, and orange starfish, and less benevolent, dark, moray eels.

If you want to explore the area on foot, over on the left-hand side of the Gulf you will find a short, easy footpath that follows deep grooves of calcareous rock. It leads on to another small inlet bordered by a shoreline of gravel and small pebbles protected on the landward side by a deep cavern.

On returning from Cape Tenta, we follow the road to Palékastro, which we abandon every time we find a sign pointing in the direction of a beach (the Greek signs contain the word *paralia*).

The first of these (about 2.5 km from the junction for Vài and Itanos) is **Maridàti.** The beach can be reached by driving along a dirt road, flanked by olive trees, that traverses (for about 1.5 km) a well-irrigated area known as the *Valley of Colours*. The high rock walls on either side of the dried-up riverbed in fact have a distinct mauve colour. Enclosed by a barrier of tamerisk trees, Maridàti is a solitary, spacious beach covered with pebbles and apparently frequented only by campers. The sea is very clean and inviting.

On returning to the main road, after a few kilometres there is another sign that indicates **Koureménos Bay**. Here, there is a small harbour filled with small fishing vessels and a long, sandy, almost ochre-colour beach, which is also surrounded by tamerisk trees. Koureménos is exposed to the strong northerly winds and is therefore a favourite spot for windsurfers. On a day when the impetuous *meltemi* was blowing hard, we had a chance to watch some of these fast, windsurf acrobats, constantly ready to adapt their coloured sails with extraordinary skill to the force and direction of the wind. Some of them go out to the tip of the Kastri promontory and then sail over to the Grandes islet. Along the road that runs parallel to the strand we noticed a good choice of attractive apartments.

Palékastro is just a few kilometres father on. This is the last eastern outpost on the island of Crete: a small town, not particularly attractive from the architectural point of view perhaps, but tranquil

*Gulf of Tenta*

and quiet enough to leave us with lasting memories of its silence and the peaceful mornings we spent there, having breakfast with yogurt and honey in one of the many *kafeneia* in the main street.

On this occasion, we spent the night at Angathià. This tiny village is less than one kilometre from Palékastro, and located on a hill that overlooks the sea. Here, we see more of the never-completed, multi-storey dwelling houses: eyesores that increasingly mar the Cretan land-scape. They are however alternated with skilful restorations of old stone houses, that instil a faint glimmer of hope that in future the architectural exploitation of the island may occur on the basis of wiser criteria.

Angathià is protected on the eastern side by intersecting conical-shaped highland formations that form part of the Petzofas chain. Its seaward outlet is at **Chiona**, a broad, sand-bordered inlet with no leisure facilities. Along the strand, shade is provided by a long row of tamerisk trees with their fine fronds that might remind one of fish scales. These trees manage to grow quite happily in the saline-rich soil and absorb water that filters in from the sea. The landward area around Chiona is green and covered with olive groves which confer a pleasant rural tone, while along the coast there are attractive tavernas spe-cialised in seafood specialities that offer romantic views across to the Kastri headland and the rocky Grandes islet.

We leave Palékastro early in the morning, when it is still silent and deserted. We intend to drive on towards the south-eastern part of the island to explore the beaches there. The landscape begins to open up, and is covered with extensive olive groves. It is bordered on the northern side by the ridge of a high mountain range and to the south by barren hills traversed by deep ravines that lead down to the sea. Our first excursion will be to the **Hohlakiès** gorge, which leads into the bay of Karoumes. After seven kilometres we arrive at the village of Hohlakliès, which is a group of whitewashed, one-storey houses that line a few narrow streets. We reflect for a moment on the sad history of this village, which was twice destroyed by the Turks: in 1821 and 1866. Passing the village, we drive on slowly amongst more olive plantations until we reach a small church, where a sign indicates the pathway that descends along the gorge. Beside the sign, a small chart provides useful geographical information and coordinates.

We put on our hiking boots and start off to explore the area. We pass by the ruins of an abandoned village to our right (perhaps the remains of the 19th-century Hohlakliès) and walk along a dried-up riverbed, which collects the water that seeps down from the nearby hills and mountains only during the wintertime. The gorge gets wider and then becomes narrow again as we proceed between the steep walls of rock, looking for an easy way through. We walk through oleander groves and brush past wild sage and the now dry origanum, which release their fragrance. Here and there, we find a few enormous, solitary and very ancient olive trees that seem to convey a sense of 'tiredness', their trunks contorted into a wild mesh of branches and cavities. Beneath their fronds appear little groups of goats here and there. After a good half hour, the walk gets easier. We reach a vast, barren, sandy area filled with prickly esparto grass. The terrain however is revived by the colour of the long, gaudy violet spikes of the hemptree (*agnus castus*) plant with its palmate leaves. We then reach the bay, which has a semi-circular form and is 'closed' at both ends by cavernous, calcareous rock with a soft, light beige colour. The beach is composed of attractive, reddish, green and ivory-colour pebbles of various sizes, all of which are fancily decorated with fine white, horizontal and vertical veins. Close to the sea, the almost perfect geometrical grid gets smaller and smaller until it seems to dissolve into fine, Havana-brown sand. The sea is welcoming but very deep just below the sandbar. It can be accessed more easily at the west end of the beach, where there are tall leafy tamerisk trees and cavities in the imposing rock faces. Here, we noticed some wild capers with their round, fleshy leaves. At the eastern end, the rock is bare and indented and rises towards a karstic landscape. Very few people seem to come here. Only in the late morning, from the bottom of the canyon, do we finally see a little group of tourists. They are suffering from the heat and hurry to dive into the beautiful, uncontaminated sea. We would categorise this excursion as being of average difficulty and we would advise you to take with you a supply of water and some food. It takes about an hour to complete on foot.

*Hohlakiés*

To visit the dark **Kato Zàkros** beach we would propose a pleasant alternative to driving. The excursion we have in mind will let you explore the '**Gorge of the Dead**' before you walk down to the sea, and on the way you can visit the archaeological site on the hill where the Minoan palace of Kato Zàkros once stood. In a lay-by on the left-hand side of the road, just a few kilometres after the village of Zàkros, a tourist information panel will show you where you can start walking down into the canyon.

Equipped with sturdy hiking boots and a water canteen, we enter a narrow valley, at the bottom of which there is a small stream. In the springtime, one would have to wade through it. We notice that it is important to keep to the left under the tall pink rock face because that is where the track is.

As we walk down the slope, we pass through large patches of yellow asphodels, which thin out as we continue into the deep, narrow valley. We pass by wild oleander, origanum (not yet in bloom but already very fragrant), small, delicate white buttercups, and even a beautiful exemplar of the Cretan Birthwort (*aristolochia cretica*. We often notice specimens of the dragon lily (*dracunculus vulgaris Schott*), one of which creates an obstacle as we proceed through the gorge. This plant, which has an almost disturbingly large flower with purple-reddish borders that regally emerge from a light-green spathe, is a typical Cretan species. It blooms in May and emanates quite an unpleasant odour. Quite common in and around human settlements, its existence is mentioned in records dating far back into the past, and painted images of the plant have been found amongst the decorations of a number of Minoan sarcophagi. After walking on for about an hour, the impressive walls of the gorge start to close in, but then we suddenly walk out into a large open space, full of more oleanders and tall bushes.

We cross the bed of the stream, hopping over some loose stepping stones, and find we have reached the entrance to the Minoan site of Kato Zàkros. At this important archaeological area, which is located on a small hill, some rare finds were uncovered almost intact under a layer of ash and lava. The site would bear out the hypothesis that the Minoan cities and palaces were destroyed by earthquakes and seaquakes and a subsequent eruption of the volcano at Santorini.

Kato Zàkros is not a village in the true sense: it has only a few houses and a few tavernas along a road shaded by eucalyptus trees that follows the contour of a long beach with course, dark sand.

Although one can easily get here by car, the locality seemed a very remote and suggestive place. Perhaps this sensation is caused by the presence of the deep gorge close to it and the archaeological site,

*Xeròkampos*

which envelops it with a special atmosphere.

We drive back towards Zàkros and, just before we reach the village, a road sign on the left indicates Xeròcambos (10 km farther on). This dirt road, which we have known for many years, has been recently widened, but it is still a very dusty route that winds on as far as **Xerò-cambos,** passing vineyards and olive plantations in a valley above a steep ravine. Although the locality is still quite a modest place, the beaches are simply wonderful. We follow the first sign pointing towards the beach and drive over to a strand with flat, calcareous rocks that slope away gradually into the sea. There are very few bathers and it is very quiet. Under the tamerisk trees at the edge of the beach, between some esparto grass and the sand, we notice the first sea lilies of the end of August, with their tender, white and light-blue corollas. It would be a crime to inadvertently step on them. There are other treasures in store at this site: on the promontory that faces south, you will find an abandoned archaeological area, which was the site of an ancient Doric city. Traces of the perimeter of dwelling houses are clearly visible, and a variety of ancient fragments may emerge if you dig a little below the surface. On the other side of the headland, called Kavalli, there is an extensive strip of light sand that slopes down into shallow water, where both adults and children can easily swim. Just

*Agia Irini*

outside the village, towards the west, along a dirt road that winds along the coast for about 1 km you will find more small inlets bordered by sand or pebbles.

We decide to spend a few hours by the sea and choose one of these inlets surrounded by tamerisk trees. We dive into the water and explore the low caverns and a large rock protruding from the water, where a solitary fisherman is spending the morning. Farther on, there is a natural harbour, where a few wooden boats are moored, and a small inlet, where we notice a few nudists swimming in the sea. The panorama here is certainly not monotonous. A group of small rocky islets in front of the Kavalli headland seem to withhold the force of the Libyan Sea.

A truly 'well-hidden' beach that is quite difficult to find is the one at **Agia Irini**. To get there from Xeròcambos, you will have to drive along the new road (with its countless bends) that connects Žiros to the south-eastern part of the island, passing by the military sites, and continuing as far as the junction, where a sign points in the direction of Kalò Choriò (3 km farther on).

From this village, we continue along the dirt road, which passes olive groves and low vineyards, and then, getting farther and farther away from the houses, the surrounding vegetation becomes more sparse and the landscape more rocky and arid, until we reach a junction. From here, we decide to risk continuing in the seaward direction even if a "T" sign (which normally indicates a 'no through road') makes us pause to reflect. Every 100 yards or so, we come across dogs with a sad, wild appearance that are chained up at the edges of the road. These poor creatures - evidently the desperate guardians of nearby flocks and herds - are obliged to spend the whole day here under the blazing sun, and a rusty, upturned, metal drum is their only shelter and source of solace.

We now see the inlet. The final descent is through a steep, narrow and quite difficult gorge. We have to leave the car just before the end as a gate bars our way, and in any case the few remaining yards between this point and the inlet are covered with oleanders. Above us, there are bizarre, looming rocks and enormous cavities created by gradual erosion, through which we can see the blue of the sky. The rock walls gradually get narrower and very soon we reach the sea. As we walk onto the beach the sun is setting: for quite some time, it seems abandoned. A fishing boat lying at anchor close to the shore, with the words Agia Irini (Saint Irene) reassures us we have reached our destination. A humble, one-storey, concrete building, which, judging from a heap of bottles stacked outside, is a bar of some kind, stands in the shade of a pair of tamerisk trees.

The shore is covered in gravel and tiny pebbles as far as the sandbar and beyond, causing a brightness and transparency typical of shorelines with a rock or pebble-strewn bottom. We dive into the water, which is flanked on both sides by high cliffs and caverns. Just a hundred yards in front of us there is a flat holm called Nisì Kipo. After swimming a short distance in this crystalline water (already a kind of metallic blue on account of the fading light), on the right, we come across a large, majestic-looking, circular cavern. Inside, it resembles an aquarium and the large rocks at the bottom suggest it might be an octopus's den. Again, this is total solitude, and the sensation of being so far removed from the rest of the world will remain in our memories. On returning, the kilometre-counter showed we were only 8 km away from the junction for Zìros.

Chrissi

# The southern beaches: from Ieràpetra to the Gulf of Goùdouras

The city of Ieràpetra does not really have a beach in the true sense, but one of its main attractions is the possibility of visiting the famous island of **Chrissì,** located eight sea miles off the mainland. The ferry-boat takes 1.5 hrs to get there. Chrissì resembles certain Caribbean islands on account of its very fine sand and the transparency of its shallow water. Other attractions are a forest of ancient Lebanese cedar trees and fossils found in volcanic rock formations. During the Byzantine period, the island was an important centre for the salt trade and a source of purple colorant. The latter product, obtained by grinding murex seashells, was once a much sought after commodity for fabrics destined for use by kings and emperors all across Europe on account of the symbolic meanings attributed to dark red and purple.

But Chrissì is always crowded. It is almost impossible to enjoy such beauty in solitude, and, for us, the idea was reinforced on the first day of June, which marks the opening of the tourist season. Close to the quay at Vagiou Mati however, a magnificent footpath winds through the sand dunes and fragrant shrubs with needle-like leaves, crosses the island and leads to the bay of Belegrina and the splendid adjacent beaches of Hatzivolakàs and Kataprosopos. These beaches are spacious and open, and allow one to avoid the modern beach umbrellas and deck chairs and laze in the natural shade of the cedars. We felt strangely conditioned by the necessity to catch the last boat back to the mainland, which leaves at five o'clock sharp: we were unable to enjoy the dusk and evening quiet in this Garden of Eden now protected by strict European laws.

The long beaches to the east of Ieràpetra are not always provided with tourist amenities and not many people visit them. They are com-

Agia Fotià

posed of dark, course sand mixed with gravel and pebbles of various sizes and colours (green, ochre or simply black and white). Most of them are finely 'decorated' with a surprising variety of natural patterns: these beaches are a real treasure-trove for those who love to collect pebbles and rocks. After such pleasant localities as Ferma, Koutsouràs, Makrìgialos and Anàlipsi the strands extend as far as Goùdouras, the southern-most point of the island, and along the way there is no lack of enchanting inlets, many of which are definitely worth visiting.

**Agia Fotià** has been famous since antiquity. A beautiful drawing produced by Francesco Basilicata in 1618 (*Spiaggia di Santa Lucia*) also clearly shows the contour of the gulf between two mountains. Surrounded by trees at the point where a river enters the sea, it is sheltered on the western side by the *Peristera* rock. Basilicata would not have been interested in this site as a holiday resort - an unknown concept in those days - but rather for what it could offer as a landing-place for utility boats (*prode e copani*).

The Agia Fotià beach (15.5 km after Ieràpetra) is indicated by a sign on the right-hand side of a bend on the main road (close to a sign indicating the Eden Rock hotel, which is just in front). From this point, a steep, narrow road descends between some vegetable gardens towards a bay divided into two sections by a riverbed. In the first part, umbrellas and deck chairs have been set out along the strand, and there is a taverna and bar (where the music is actually quite good!) The second half is 'free', and in the summer ample shade is provided by the tall tamerisk trees. If you're looking for company, Agia Fotià is an ideal place to be: many young people come here in the afternoon, and in July and August, volley ball matches are often organised. The seabed slopes down into deep water after just a few yards, and the water is crystal clear. Guided underwater tours are also offered at this site.

We do not live in this part of the island but we like to spend a day here at least once a year to enjoy the undeniable charm of the Libyan Sea: with a soft drink at the bar or an Italian espresso coffee or enjoying a simple plate of fried fish and a rich Greek salad at the taverna by the large car park. In particular, we enjoy the happy atmosphere created by the presence of so many young people.

If you're looking for some peace and quiet, the small bay of **Galìni** (the next inlet towards the east) may be more to your liking. It has a sandy beach and tourist amenities. Yet another site worth visiting is the small beach at **Diaskari,** located close to Anàlipsi, just after the village in the bay of **Makrìgialos**. The attractions here are the shady tamerisk trees, a few coves and a decent bar where rooms can be rented.

*Makrìgialos*

The small island of **Koufonìssi**, an ancient Roman site with the remains of a theatre, an aqueduct and double harbour, is well worth visiting. Like at Chrissì, the shellfish on this island were once a source of purple colorant. The trade was however abandoned around 400 AD, when Koufonìssi was attacked by invaders, who burnt and destroyed the city and demolished all of its statues. Only in summer and only once a week, a ferryboat from Makrìgialos takes people to visit the golden beaches and crystal clear-waters of this locality. If the heat is not too intense (there are no trees on this island), you may want to visit the southern headland, where, according to travellers who came here centuries ago, there were once the impressive ruined fragments of the colossal statue of an emperor, the base of which was later used to build the old lighthouse. Koufonìssi is also a favourite hermit's haunt: from the 15th to the 17th century, the caverns of the western promontory were inhabited by anchorites and, it is said, there is still one hermit left.

We start off again on the national highway, which, at the junction for the **Kapsà** monastery, gets narrower and becomes a rural road that winds between canebrakes and olive groves and continues along the coast between the sea and rocks with an anthracite colour. The monastery, which dates back to the 15th century, is ensconced on a peak and faces the eastern margin of the Perivolàkia gorge. It is a popular destination for Christians as a monk called Gerontogiannis, to

*Near Kapsà monastery*

whom various miracles were attributed, lived here in the 1800s. Another spot which not many people know about is the Perivolàkia canyon (3.5 km long), which can be visited in about two and a half hours. The up-and-down route, which winds on between a series of crags, includes a point where one has to climb up a ladder to get to a higher level. In spring, halfway along the gorge, the water present at the bottom of a little valley creates a waterfall, which explains the presence of a variety of aromatic plants, such as wild sage, savory and thyme. There are also oleander trees, oaks and endemic flower species such as Cretain Sainfoin (*ebenus cretica*), catmint (*nepeta*), and pink-coloured cress (*ricotia cretica*). The walk ends at the village of Kato Pervolakia, at an altitude of 600 m above sea level. If you decide to go back on foot along the same route, be careful as you go as the descent is not so easy; but once you return to the point below the monastery, a small glade filled with tamerisk trees and a small rocky inlet will allow you to rest for a while.

We finally reach the Gulf of **Goùdouras**, a small urban centre full of greenhouses. There are a few good tavernas here that serve excellent seafood, but it is not exactly the best place in Crete to go for a swim. The coast road ends here and turns inland to wind northwards through the green hills, crossing the island in the direction of Sitìa.

# SUMMARY OF BEACHES LISTED IN THIS GUIDE

## LEGEND
### ROUTE

Beach accessible only by boat

Beach accessible only by boat on foot:
long excursion (over 15 mins)

Beach accessible only on foot:
short excursion (less than 15 mins)

Beach accessible by car on a section of dirt road

Beach accessible by car

### AMENITIES

Free beach with no facilities

Free beach with no facilities, but with
refreshments and shade

Beach with limited facilities: umbrellas,
deck chairs, refreshments

Beach with facilities: umbrellas, deck chairs,
showers, sports, bar, refreshments

### TYPE OF BEACH

Beach with fine sand

Beach with course sand/gravel

Pebble beach

Small beach with rocks and direct access to the sea

# WESTERN CRETE

## The beaches facing the Libyan Sea: from Hòra Sfakìon on to Elafonissi

| Beach | Access | Amenities | Sea |
|---|---|---|---|
| Hòra Sfakìon | 🚗 | ⛱ ♨ 🍴 | ••• |
| Ilingas beach | 🚗 | ☀ | ••• |
| Glikà Nera | 🥾 | ☀ 🥤 | ••• |
| Phinix | ⚓ | ⛱ 🍴 | ••• |
| Marmara | 🥾 | ☀ | •• |
| Agios Paulos | 🥾 | ☀ | ••• |
| Agia Rouméli | 🥾 | ⛱ ♨ 🍴 | ••• |
| Sougia | 🚗 | ⛱ ♨ 🍴 | ••• |
| lissos | 🥾 | ☀ | ••• |
| Gianiskàri beach | 🚙 | ⛱ ♨ 🍴 | ••• |
| Gianiskàri sandy beach | 🚙 | ⛱ 🥤 | ≈ |
| Paleòchora | 🚗 | ⛱ ♨ 🍴 | ≈ |
| Grammeno Votsalo beach | 🚗 | ⛱ 🥤 | ••• |
| Krios beach | 🚗 | ⛱ ♨ 🍴 | ≈ |
| Elafonìssi beach | 🚗 | ⛱ ♨ 🍴 | ≈ |
| Elafonìssi: the Cedar Beach | 🥾 | ☀ | ≈ |

## The beaches in the far west: from Gramvousa to Chrisoskalitìissa

| Beach | Access | Amenities | Sea |
|---|---|---|---|
| Gramvousa: Balos beach | 🥾 | ☀ | ≈ |
| Phalàssarna | 🚗 | ⛱ 🥤 | ≈ |
| Sfinàri | 🚗 | ⛱ 🥤 | ••• |
| Amigdalokefàli beach | 🚗 | ☀ | ~ |
| Agios Mìronas | 🚗 | ☀ | •• |

## The beaches at Kissamo and Hania: from the Rodopoù peninsula to the bay of Kalives

| Beach | Access | Amenities | Sea |
|---|---|---|---|
| Rodopoù: Ravdoucha | 🚗 | ☀ | •• |
| Rodopoù: Dìktynna | 🚙 | ☀ | ••• |
| Koutallas | 🚗 | ⛱ 🥤 | ••• |
| Obròsgialos beach | 🚗 | ☀ 🥤 | ~ |
| Almirìda | 🚗 | ⛱ ♨ 🍴 | ≈ |
| Stavròs | 🚗 | ⛱ ♨ 🍴 | ≈ |
| Kalathàs | 🚗 | ⛱ ♨ 🍴 | ≈ |
| Maràthi | 🚗 | ⛱ ♨ 🍴 | ≈ |

# CENTRAL CRETE

## The beaches to the west of Ierapetra: from Mìrtos to Agios Nikòlaos

Mìrthos

Vàthos

Kallikovratis

Tertsa

Arvi

Tsoùtsouras

Agios Nikitas

Maridaki

## The beaches to the west of Ieràpetra: from Mìrtos to Agios Nikòlaos

Tris Ekklisìes

Tripiti

## The beaches from Màtala to Lendas

Màtala

Kokkìni Ammos beach

Agiofàrango

Martsàlo

Vathì

Kalì Liménes

Chrisòstomo

Platìa Peràmata

Loutra

Lentas

Limanaki beach

Dytikòs

## The beaches to the west of Ieràpetra: from Mìrtos to Agios Nikita

Agia Galìni

Ammoùdi

Agia Fotinì

Ligres

Tris Petres

Agios Paulos

Dìplono Petres

Agios Ioannis (Agia Galini)

Kokkinos Pirgos

Kalamaki

Kommos

## The beaches from Préveli to Frankocàstello

Préveli

Damnòni

Koràka

Frangokàstello

## The northern beaches: from Malia to Réthimno

Malia

Hersònissos

Amnisos

Lygarià

Agia Pelagìa

Aliki

Almyrida

Balì

Pànormo

Georgioùpoli

# EASTERN CRETE

## The beaches at Elounda

Kolokìtha

Plaka

Agios Ioannis

## The beaches of the Gulf of Mirabello

Kitroplatìa

Almiròs

Ammoudàra

Karavostàsi

Agios Pantaléimon

Voulisma

Thòlos

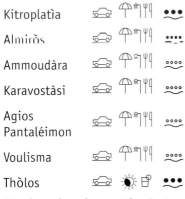

## Northern beaches on the Cretan SeaNord

Vlihàdia

Agios Andreas

Anògia

Mìlatos

Sissi

## The beaches near Sitìa on the eastern coast

Vai

Erimoùpoli

Tenta, gulf of

Maridàti

Koureménos

Chiona

Hohlakiés

Kato Zakros

Xeròkampos

Agia Irini

## The beaches facing the Libyan Sea: from Ieràpetra to Goùdouras

Chrissì

Agia Fotià

Galini

Diaskari

Kapsà beach

Koufonìssi

Ieràpetra beach

# Index of Place-names

Michele Buonsanti - Alberta Galla

# CANDIA VENEZIANA

## VENETIAN ITINERARIES THROUGH CRETE

A guide to the historical remains of the Venetian dominion

MYSTIS
EDITIONS

DI CANDIA

CITTÀ
VECCHIA

MYSTIS

ANTONIS ALIBERTIS

Hail, King Minos!

MYSTIS
EDITIONS

ANTONIS VASILAKIS

CRETE

GUIDE

Alibertis Antonis

Follow us
In the GORGE of
SAMARIA

A world of Nature, Life,
Legend and History

MYSTIS
EDITIONS

MYSTIS